Step It Up

How French women hack work-life balance

Step It Up

How French women hack work-life balance

By Géraldine Le Meur

with Anaïs Bon

To Arthur, Gauthier, and Grégoire

Contents

Preface

Like all those who have been lucky enough to meet Géraldine, whether in the course of their private or professional lives, I feel a mixture of genuine warmth and sincere admiration for Géraldine. Her personality and life path—both on the banks of the Seine or in the heart of Silicon Valley—command respect. I am deeply honored to be associated with the inspirational work she has undertaken by writing this book.

I firmly believe that all forms of diversity are a fantastic and unlimited source of wealth for individuals and for businesses. And today, attitudes are changing. As a business leader, I have noticed a fundamental shift in mindset within my own company, but also within the world at large. Diversity, equality and parity are no longer vague quasi-mystical objectives; they are now demanded by all our shareholders, our own employees and consumers first and foremost. We must now transpose this dynamic into the sphere of entrepreneurial initiative.

The testimonials so diligently brought together in these pages will convince each and every one of you that there should be no barriers to entrepreneurial liberty, whether in terms of class, age, personal situation, or nationality. Nor any related to gender. The greatest obstacles to creative energy are often the ones women impose upon themselves.

The 30 well-known women you will meet in this book will inspire and liberate you. You're holding in your hands a tremendous concentration of ambition and determination; a plea in favor of action and creation—the very first steps along your own path to personal and professional success.

Alexandre Ricard
CEO of Pernod Ricard

Introduction

Recently, a close friend of mine pointed out that I was an exception, with my three sons, my entrepreneurial background, my choice of expatriation. He said that made me a "model." I had a visceral reaction to his words, completely refusing the image. "No, I am not an exception. There is nothing special about me. I am just me, with my life and my choices." This book grew from a desire to share just that, to share with other women, with you, this capacity we all have to be exceptional to others, and yet so normal to ourselves.

Albert Einstein said, "Life is like riding a bicycle. To keep your balance, you must keep moving." For a very long time, I thought I knew how to ride. I followed my path without asking too many questions, sure that I was pedaling at the right pace to keep my balance. Then, recently, a divorce unsettled many of my personal and professional certainties. I shifted to mountain biking on a trail scattered with rocks. I realized how important it was to surround yourself with the right people, to share, to discuss, and to set a direction. You need some luck to find a circle of benevolent support, and it is not always easy to dare to call yourself into question. By collecting the testimonials of women whom I admire, most of whom are friends (real ones, not Facebook friends), I want to create an inspiring and motivating environment for other women, not to give lessons or to set some glamorous expectations.

What does it mean to be a woman entrepreneur in real life? Today, the lens focuses on startups, tech, and unicorns, but is that really what it is all about? Entrepreneurship is a mindset, a lifestyle. It's about stepping up your life and career, moving it toward who you really want to be. For women, it's even more challenging, as you have to find the right rhythm at every stage.

There is also a cultural dimension. I have been living in the United for almost 12 years now, and the more I get to call San Francisco home, the more I realize there are cultural differences. I want to share the perspective of French business women not only with tech entrepreneurs, but with women who choose to lead their personal lives and careers differently, in a very entrepreneurial way.

In short, the idea was to write a mentor-book. Today, young women need inspiring role models who open doors for them, be it to start a business or more generally deploy their full potential. It is true that we see impressive women on the covers of magazines. Yet, are we really able to identify with those glossy icons? It is a little like trying on some clothing we see in an ad—you find the right size, but you don't look like the model in the picture. There is only one Michelle Obama and only one Sheryl Sandberg. They are very inspiring in many ways, and yet the world is full of women whose exemplary lives can serve as examples. Not everyone seeks to become a public figure. There are other models of success, some perhaps less visible, but no less impressive nor ambitious.

I want to demystify entrepreneurship, to reveal how French women create a path to success and, more generally, explore the idea of professional and personal success. I hope that in each of these testimonials you will find nuggets of inspiration that give you impetus and light up your path. Role models serve this purpose, offering modest landmarks that cause us to pause and ask if we agree, and perhaps leading us to coarse correct if needed. The power of example can help you to assess yourself and check that you are truly on the path that is your own. This is not about doing well based on some external standards, but rather on doing right by your own line of conduct. This is not about forcing your way into a box, but about finding your path. To do so, many of the women you will meet in these pages have joyfully left the beaten path.

Stepping up to your life

One of my favorite expressions in a professional context is certainly, "little brooks make great rivers." It applies to so many situations, whether I'm going through a hard time managing expenses or on the starting block to climb an apparently insurmountable mountain. On numerous occasions, team members have told me how this approach has helped them. And it is true for women—by changing small things, we can accomplish great things.

We are all different, and that is what makes us exceptional. Everyone can find their path. Everyone can create the extraordinary from their ordinary. Everyone has the resources to express their full potential and live their dreams. What remains is to be truly conscious of this capacity, and that is a whole other matter. We each need to roll up our sleeves and identify our strengths, recognize them and use them as our foundation.

All women are strong. They just need to find their own particular tools to implement what they want to do. None of us are wonder women—not even the most brilliant among us. It is important to demystify success, and particularly entrepreneurial success, so that it appears to be what it really is—accessible.

Everything in my entrepreneurial adventure seemed normal. Things unfolded, with requisite amounts of sweat and stress, quite naturally. I had to invent it all. I grew my companies organically, and when I created the first one we were not talking about venture capital to finance it. And I'm still a big believer that your first investor is your first paying customer.

We all have an entrepreneurial nature just waiting to be cultivated to flower and bear fruit. Women are polymorphous creators. This book talks a lot about entrepreneurship, as it is the path I followed and that I know the best. However, it is not meant to fall into a dogma of encouraging everyone to step up to be an entrepreneur, but rather to step up to your life. What is important is finding your place, defining your possibilities, and discovering what you need to succeed.

The time of modest women has passed. It is my hope that the practical advice and real stories that follow give you the boost you need to step closer to your dreams.

Chapter 1
Half the World

Beyond the battle of the sexes

> *Women who seek to be equal with men*
> *lack ambition.*
>
> Timothy Leary

Things are changing in the United States, but still quite recently women in tech had to not only compete with men, but be sure to win. I have met many brilliant women who established themselves in opposition to men with every intention of showing them up. At the same time, I have met others, like a young woman at a conference who was married to a Silicon Valley entrepreneur, choosing to be a stay-at-home mom after having been a prosecutor and having paid for her brilliant husband's studies.

Yet, since 2017 and the start of the Me Too movement, we have been experiencing an unprecedented fracture that will most certainly leave scars. It could, however, allow us to move forward. Women startup founders looking for funding have accused certain venture capitalists of abuse of power, leading some to make public apologies. Accusations of sexual harassment and sexism have pushed some key players out of Silicon Valley. Despite the consecutive firing of 20 employees, Susan Fowler's revelations about unacceptable practices at Uber led to the ouster of CEO Travis Kalanick in June 2017.

Already in 2015, a survey of entrepreneurial women in Silicon Valley revealed that 60 percent had been victims of sexual harassment. The problem is all the more acute in the tech world, where labor laws do not cover relations between investors and founders, and where the boundaries between professional and personal are not always clear, with meetings that run late in bars or at home. Frédérique Dame, who has lived in the United States since 2000, has had a fine career in Silicon Valley, standing out as a product leader at Uber from 2012 to 2016, after having worked at SmugMug, Photobucket, and Yahoo. As a woman working in tech, she insists on the importance of always setting very clear boundaries and surrounding yourself with people who are on your side. In our interview on February 16, 2018, she said, "I have always done what I have to in order to avoid ambiguous situations. I feel like my grandmother when I say that, but it's a reality. I never wear a low-cut top for a meeting and never accept a professional appointment in a hotel bar. I always try to stay in a work context. Similarly, I learned to never take anything personally. If someone doesn't take me seriously, that is their problem. I go find people who see my true value and with whom I can work as an equal."

I feel reassured now that the violence of 2017 and #metoo surge has passed, that deep changes are taking place to bring more inclusion and diversity. Emily Chang's book *Brotopia* has contributed to the changes by kicking the Silicon Valley anthill.

Things need shaking up, as women still only play an anecdotal role. There are historical reasons for the gender unbalance. In the 1960s and 1970s, the computer industry lacked skilled workers. Two psychologists, William Cannon and Dallis Perry, set out to develop a personality test to identify good programmers. After studying a panel of around 1,200 men and 200 women, they came to the conclusion that good programmers didn't like people. These tests had a huge influence and were used by companies for years. If you were looking for asocial people, you were more likely to recruit men than women. There is no proof that an asocial man is a better programmer than a woman, but this stereotype dies hard. Silicon Valley has a direct influence on the way people throughout the world think, communicate and consume. That is why it is so important to restore a balance in the tech world, because tech impacts society as a whole. It can, and should, set an example.

I find Susan Wojcicki to be very inspiring, as CEO of YouTube and mother of five children. She leads a top-tier tech business and remains remarkably simple. She believes that her professional life and her personal life mutually benefit each other, a philosophy I wholly adopt. Her responsibilities do not keep her from being at home at 6 p.m. every evening to have dinner with her children. She took a stand against gender discrimination in Silicon Valley, which can take many forms such as being frequently interrupted, or being ignored while attention goes to less experienced male colleagues, or having to wait for some man to recuperate your ideas for them to be considered interesting. At a Boardlist dinner I attended, Susan Wojcicki very specifically highlighted that power is not earned, but rather passed down. Women need to pass it on to other women, but men also need to pass it on to women.

Among other notable initiatives, in April 2018, a group of women investors led by Aileen Lee, ranked by Forbes among the most powerful women in the world, launched an association called All Raise, which sets out to fight for more funding for women entrepreneurs, with a very clear and simple vision: "We believe people of all different backgrounds should have the opportunity to participate, shape, and succeed in the founding, funding, and building of technology-driven companies." Together! Not women against men, or vice versa. I deeply believe in this complementarity when we can make it happen.

Being French, I realized that much remains to be done in France as well, but that we already have good foundations supporting women. We should not stop there.

Earning a place at the table

For men, likability and success are correlated. As they get more successful, more powerful, they're better liked. For women, success and likability are negatively correlated. As a woman gets more successful, more powerful, she is less liked.
—Sheryl Sandberg, COO Facebook

The place we've earned is so recent. Let's not forget that talking about women entrepreneurs is very new. In the United States women only got the right to vote in 1920, while in France they had to wait until 1944. In France, it wasn't until 1965 that women could open a bank account and sign checks without asking permission from their husband. In 1974, the United States Equal Credit Opportunity Act made it illegal to refuse a credit card to a woman based on her gender. So how could we imagine them running a business?

For a few years now, the media have been deploring the lack of women in tech. Schools have only been coed in France since the 1960s, but it was in 1972, the year I was born, that the first engineering schools in France began to accept women. In the United States, with a few exceptions, women couldn't attend Ivy League schools until 1969 at the earliest. We have so few years behind us playing a full role in the economy that it will still take a few years to create normalcy or a standard.

In March 2018, I had the pleasure of meeting Annie Combelles, the first woman to have gone to SupAéro, one of France's top aerospace engineering schools. Her professional path is simply fascinating. She navigated her entire career in a man's universe, and although she says she quickly stopped paying attention to the gender unbalance, today she is very active as a mentor in the Women Initiative Foundation, which promotes the advancement of women in the workplace. Annie wanted to be a surgeon, but with the civil unrest in France in May 1968, her father preferred to send her to a math preparatory school. She was one of six girls out of fifty students to start off the year. Only four girls remained by the end of the first term. Her father told her to pursue her studies, so she could "become a teacher and raise her children." She didn't pass the elite teaching school entrance exam, but did get into SupAéro. There were only three women in her class. She graduated in 1973, a bad year in the aeronautics industry. She decided to join SFENA, a French aeronautics company, where she developed the first digital autopilots for Airbus, from proof of concept to certification.

"I was responsible for all the software that was piloting the planes. Four days before certification, the plane had already succeeded a number of test flights, but right before take off of the final test, the throttle control sprang back automatically. I took the heat. Someone had changed a parameter at the last minute without paying attention to the unit system needed for the data input. I was told, 'You're fired if we don't get certified.' I answered that I only worked one way, honestly. I explained that someone made an unauthorized change and that had we applied all the good practices, it would not have happened. The French certifier said, 'Her reasoning holds water, we can sign off on this.' The solution we set up at the time is still being used. I learned everything on the job."

Later she joined the French multinational Thales, where she worked on simulators, and notably on an incredibly complex nuclear reactor simulator. That was also the period (1985-1986) of the first European-funded programs. She joined a consortium and won a project focused on the reliability of onboard software, but her employer did not support her to develop it. So, she went knocking on the door of the French Atomic Energy Commission, and on July 1, 1989, decided to found an information technology consulting firm called Objectif Technologie. Her goal was to apply the good practices she used in the aeronautics industry to developing software and systems for other sectors. She set her goals and moved forward. Wanting to develop internationally, she sold her business to Q-Labs, a subsidiary of the Swedish multinational Ericsson. One thing leading to another, she took control of her business again in 2011 and renamed it Inspearit. Today, Inspearit operates in France, the Netherlands, Italy, and Asia.

Annie's example demonstrates that you can always make your way, even in a world considered to be closed to women. That said, many obstacles remain to real gender equality.

Taking France as an example, the French had to wait for 1972 for the first laws regarding equal salaries—the Equal Pay Act was signed in the United States in 1963. Although twelve other laws have followed in France, a gender pay gap of nine percent persists, according to Benjamin Griveaux, a government spokesperson who spoke at an an event organized by the Willa incubator on March 8, 2018. The further one advances in age and in the organizational hierarchy, the greater the gap. A law on male-female parity has been in force for 17 years, and yet, prior to the most recent elections, the French National Assembly counted fewer than 30 percent women, as the later were always assigned to circumscriptions that were impossible to win. While France's army may rank fourth worldwide for the number of women, that is not because France is ahead of the others in terms of equality, but rather because the others are behind.

Gender inequalities are rooted in cultural, linguistic, and historic habits and continue to feed behavioral differences, such as women having higher aversion to risk and more limited taste for competition. Professions with high levels or responsibility, where working hours are less flexible, are stragglers in terms of gender equality, because the lack of flexibility penalizes women, who continue to bear a greater load of household tasks than men, whether or not they work. This is one of the reasons that women are so little represented in professions like market finance. Female students in finance tend to get better grades than their male counterparts, but they are less likely to pursue this career path. In a November 2016 ESSEC Knowledge article, "Do gender stereotypes influence your financial decisions?", the authors François Longin and Estefania Santacreu-Vasut observed a balanced population of students, 53 percent female and 47 percent male for an entire academic year. The female students demonstrated better performance than the male students on average and had considerably better grades among the higher-grade set. However, fewer female students decided to continue finance studies: 21 versus 43. Later, with the same academic path, 41 former female students versus 76 male students worked in finance after graduating (classes from 2013-2016). Furthermore, cultural expectations regarding specific gender roles could impact the career choices women make.

In 2016, the former French government minister Fleur Pellerin founded Korelya Capital, an investment fund aimed at promoting Korean technology investment in France. When she put together her team, she received five times more resumés from men than from women. The financial sector remains primarily masculine, as does the technology sector—out of seven businesses financed by Korelya, only one was founded by a woman.

From 2010 to 2012, Fleur headed up a "think and do" tank working to promote diversity and equal opportunities. The goal was to count the women and people of non-French origin found on the boards of companies listed on the French stock market index CAC 40. The result was ridiculously low. Out of approximately 500 board members, there were a mere ten or so women. "The men say, 'We try to find women, but there is no pool to choose from, and when we do find a woman who is qualified to sit on the board, she says that it takes too much of her time and that she wouldn't be good at it.' I think men don't even ask the question," Fleur said when we interviewed her on March 7, 2018. In 2011, a law was passed in France setting a mandatory quota of 40 percent of the underrepresented gender on boards, and oddly enough, the CAC 40 companies have found that missing pool of women. The penalty for companies that do not respect the quota is especially well designed: Directors' fees are blocked. It is very effective. This quota system will soon apply to smaller businesses as well. Recently, California passed a law requiring in 2019 at least one woman on boards of directors of publicly traded companies headquartered in the state, a number that will increase by 2021.

Fleur also regretted the lack of female candidates for high-level positions in the French administration when she was minister. "When you are in the government designating the people to lead the central administrations, it is hard to say you're going to do some affirmative action if there is only one female candidate among several men and she is not convincing. Maybe that is what you should do, maybe you should say to yourself that this candidate may seem less good, but I'll push for her anyway. But those are necessarily hard decisions to make when you are heading up an administration."

Tunisian Amira Yahyaoui founded the NGO Al Bawsala ("the compass" in Arabic) to place citizens in the heart of political action in her country and to ensure the transparency of the revolution. Today, she is in the process of founding Mos.com, a startup with Expa, a startup studio founded by Garrett Camp, who also founded Uber. She is very genuine and defends her ideas with conviction. She has the courage of her opinions and a very interesting point of view concerning the role of women today. "Today, if I were given the choice to be born a man or a woman, I would choose to be a woman because I think I would have more opportunities. All my life, I've tried to turn negatives into positives," she said when I questioned her in February 2018. "Being a woman in Silicon Valley gives you more power because nobody dares to say anything to you anymore —and I make the most of that. Some people may view the Me Too movement as exaggerated and even negative, but it is just that exaggeration that gives it power. Men abused us excessively, and it is not so serious that it comes flying back in their face. We need to fight for women to have a seat at the boardroom table, even if they don't have the right skills. Often the men around the table are idiots as well. I deeply believe what French journalist Françoise Giroud said, 'Women will be the real equals of men the day when an incompetent woman will be named to a high-level position. I think that women today need to, as the Arabic expression goes, stretch out their arms and legs and sit down at the middle of the table. It is not because I don't like men that I think we should take advantage of their weakness, but rather because it is high time that balance returns, radically, and without apology. If those who have access to power don't do it, who will?"

For Amira, it is worth exaggerating today so that we move toward gender equality not by baby steps, but by making a great leap forward in time and history. In order for things to evolve just an inch in countries where women have few rights, in our countries, we need to jump miles ahead. "Today, we need to exaggerate. It's okay. We can apologize later." After all, men know how to apologize.

To her, another crucial battle is educating young boys. "My stepson is twelve years old, and I have been his stepmother since he was six and a half. It is a strong message for him to see his stepmother give conferences around the world, be on television, disagree with his father and say it out loud. It's very different than saying to him, 'You need to respect women and open the door for your sister.' Children learn through imitation, not through words." In the education that Amira received, no difference was made between her and her brothers. She only learned she was different from them when she went to school, where girls were not treated the same, such as having to wear an apron, being served less at the cafeteria, and doing gymnastics rather than playing soccer.

Finally, the third battle that women need to fight, according to Amira, is to lead in the world of money. And this is a priority. Women need to become rich. She very correctly pointed out to me that in Forbes' listing of the richest people in the world, all the women are wives, widows, heirs or daughters of rich men. It's a sad observation. Other than a few aliens such as Sheryl Sandberg, no one comes to mind spontaneously when trying to list women who have built their own fortune.

Obstacles remain, but the reign of ambitious women is here. Women need to accept to take their place, and men need to accept that we bring them something else. Millennials want to live life to the fullest. In France, 66 percent of women under 30 affirm they are ambitious, a number that drops to 45 percent after the age of thirty. Among them, 79 percent believe that society today still has a hard time accepting ambition among women.

Women Entrepreneurs

> *Sometimes women entrepreneurs are their own challenge, [in terms of] believing in themselves.*
> —Tory Burch, founder of her namesake fashion label

It's an underlying trend. In the 2010s, more and more often entrepreneurs are women. In France, they are the majority among individual business owners under the age of 30. Female entrepreneurship encompasses 163 million women who founded businesses throughout the world between 2015 and 2017, according to a Global Entrepreneurship Monitor (GEM) study. The gap with men is shrinking. In Europe, the percentage of women graduate entrepreneurs surpasses that of men. In France, 40% of business founders are women. The percentage is rising, but women remain a minority because there are still obstacles.

However, according to the mayor of Paris Anne Hidalgo, at a speech given on March 8, 2018, companies with at least one woman among the founders outperform other companies, with a return on investment that is 35 percent higher. The failure rate for women entrepreneurs is only 10 percent in developed economies, one-third less than that of men. Is it because they are more cautious? Do they wait longer to eliminate more risk before launching? Women who start their own business may have relational and organizational strengths they use with their teams. They may also be innovative. In Paris, 21 percent of tech startups are said to have been founded by women; women also see digital technology as a major advantage for entrepreneurs. Fund raising by women has increased significantly in recent years. In absolute value, French women raised 142.5 million euros in 2017, 13 percent more than in 2016, which was already 28 percent more than in 2015. However, that only represents seven percent of the total amount raised in France. Studies also reveal that entrepreneurial goals are different for men and women. Women are less concerned with power for themselves than with the freedom entrepreneurship offers, and the possibility that you have when you run a business to use all your skills. Entrepreneurship is a way for women to flourish, according to French journalist Marina Al Rubbae.

A 2015 KPMG survey revealed that 44 percent of women business leaders rose to the top of their companies because they themselves founded it or bought it. Entrepreneurship can be a way to overcome the difficulty of getting in-house promotions. Women are better represented at the head of small companies with 10 and 20 employees, although their presence is growing at the head of large companies. This is partly explained by a lack of self-confidence. Heading up a small business is less risky than leading a large corporation. Women come in first place taking up the torch of family businesses, including in some sectors that remain male bastions, such as construction. Traditionally overrepresented in the social, personal services and commerce sectors, women are increasingly targeting energy, agri-food, industry, and automotive sectors, according to Marina Al Rubbae.

Although women still struggle to impose themselves in the information, communication, and construction industries, traditionally dominated by men, they did found 48 percent of industrial companies, although mainly in jewelry and clothing, where they represent almost all the business founders. Stereotypes die hard.

Pay inequalities remain at the top of companies, with women entrepreneurs (self-employed or salaried) earning an average of 31 percent less than their male counterparts in 2015, including in the highest income brackets.

In 2018, there were 20,000 women entrepreneurs in the Paris region, but only 39 percent of companies were run by women. In a speech given on March 8, 2018, French politician Alexandra Dublanche, who heads up economic development for the Paris region, stated that twenty-seven percent of entrepreneurial women question their abilities compared to only nine percent of men. According to a 2016 Hiscox survey, 35 percent of women entrepreneurs feel less experienced than men, and 36 percent say they are afraid of failure. In 2005, women had a 30 lower chance than men to get help from banks when starting their business, Anne Hidalgo said during her speech on March 8, 2018. "Am I able to do this?' is a very feminine question. It is not enough to just commit. When we get into a position of responsibility, where we did not previously have authority, we are seen as authoritarian. Having very active networks is what allows women today to support each other. Just explaining the obstacles is liberating. The responsibility we have today is to pass on what we know, to reduce the barriers for younger women."

It is harder for women to get funding. Forty-four percent believe that business failures are due to the lack of funding. In the United States, in 2017, only two percent of the money invested in venture capital went to projects run by women.

Estefania Santacreu-Vasut and François Longin, two business school professors, developed a simulation tool called SimTrade designed to integrate social factors into financial experiments and to determine if financial markets were taking gender into account, and if investors harbored stereotypes that could influence the performance of their investments. They conducted a simulation of a solar car manufacturer about to appoint a new CEO. A random selection of male or female CEOs contextualized the trading experience in a gender-sensitive social environment. When a woman was named CEO in the simulation, female traders reacted more favorably to this announcement. On the contrary, male traders had a more negative reaction. When a male CEO was appointed, the results were the opposite. It seemed particularly important that the appointed CEO and the trader be of the same sex, a phenomenon called "homophilia"— interconnections tend to be more frequent among similar individuals. According to the researchers, network formation plays an important role in the long-term persistence of homophilia. This shows how important it is to develop diversity throughout the entire entrepreneurial ecosystem, from investment funds to the press and speakers at conferences.

Caroline Ramade began her career as a journalist. After working in political communication for elected officials, she turned digital. When she began working for the City of Paris, she took over the departments responsible for digital services, innovation and relations with startups. She watched the emergence of the ecosystem of Parisian startups. Today, Caroline is founding the startup 50inTech, a crowdsourcing platform that sets out to help women entrepreneurs to succeed, but when we spoke in October 2017, she was managing director of the incubator Paris Pionnières, which is now called Willa, where she set herself the mission of promoting female entrepreneurship. "There are still obstacles in our education we need to overcome, especially with regard to ambition and risk-taking. Female entrepreneurs face problems of harassment. In startups, women display their ambition when pushing a project that is important to them, but hear investors ask if they will have children. They do not perceive themselves as victims, which is normal, but when we ask, we realize that the question of children and marriage is omnipresent. Women do not necessarily perceive this as harassment, but there are visible gender biases that occur. There is another gender bias related to sectors that men do not take seriously. Yoga, for example, represents a huge market of several billions of euros, but gives rise to a very strong condescension on the part of men. There are many opportunities for growth in areas that have not yet been invented.

At the age of 31, Clementine Piazza made the jump to entrepreneurship, creating InMemori, a startup we hosted at The Refiners, the seed fund and program I founded in 2016 with Carlos Dias and Pierre Gaubil. InMemori allows people who have just lost a loved one to gather relatives and friends in a private online area that provides various services to pay one's respects. Our interview took place in December 2017, at the very beginning of the first round of fundraising. Venture capital remains a man's world, and Clementine noted that she faced three challenges as a woman—prejudices, projections, and fear. In some areas, we are obliged to be better than men. For example, in the fundraising process, a woman needs to know her numbers better than a man. Clementine was systematically questioned about the barriers to entry, while she had no questions about her marketing and growth strategy. "I didn't feel convincing when it came to barriers to entry. We have to deal with projections. I know who I am, but I play with what I project to others. If I'm not sure of myself, I look too weak, while if I look too sure of myself, I come off as arrogant, and if I'm reserved, I look anxious. You have to be extremely aware of others' perceptions and drive them. Women have to constantly develop accuracy of tone."

When investors (including women) interview startup founders, they do not ask men and women the same questions. They ask men about the potential for gain, and women about the potential for loss. In a 2017 article in TechCrunch written by Connie Loizos, Aileen Lee, one of the few female figures of venture capital in Silicon Valley, advises female founders looking to convince investors to appear confident, but not arrogant, and especially not too shy. She stresses the importance of knowing the numbers inside and out, as prejudices make it much more difficult for women to be taken as seriously than men. Aileen Lee also encourages founders to connect with other women, entrepreneurs, and investors.

Ever since Céline Lazorthes's parents installed an Internet connection in their home when she was 14, she has been obsessed with working on the Web. She studied computer project management at a top French engineering school specialized in the field of computer science and software engineering. Then she studied management and new technologies at business school. In 2004, she worked for the online bank ING Direct, heading up all online communication on the Orange savings account. This experience familiarized her with innovation in banking as well as the importance of the customer journey. Celine organized a fundraiser for a student weekend and Leetchi, now the leading online fund pool in Europe, was born. This was late 2007 early 2008. Céline graduated in the middle of the subprime crisis. Paradoxically, the crisis context was very favorable; the lack of job offers encouraged her to found a business. Céline was very young and did not look much like a banker. When the banking markets in France opened up to competition, it took her two and a half years to get a banking license, which she obtained in December 2012.

The situation was complex. The minority status of women in tech was also an advantage, especially in terms of visibility. The obstacles remained very internal, Céline explained in our interview on December 11, 2017. "Many people wanted to give a helping hand. I made appointments with investors who spoke only to my partner, but that was marginal. Now that I'm investing in projects, I see that women are less confident and take more limited risks. It must be said and repeated that it is possible. It's not a question of age or experience, but of self-assurance. We also had a woman chief technology officer (Laure Nemée). This helped us a lot to attract other female profiles and to recruit more open-minded men." For Marion Carrette, the founder of Zilok and OuiCar, who we interviewed on the same day, being a woman has been a major asset. As there were not many women entrepreneurs, she enjoyed significant media visibility which she took advantage of.

Fanny Bouton, expert consultant in new media and organizer of Fanny's Party, the rendezvous of the Parisian geeks, works in tech, which is a very masculine professional environment. Initially, there was an overwhelming majority of men at her parties, but Fanny had the feeling that they took care of her and supported her. She never had the impression of having to break through glass ceilings, and rather benefited from the kindness of men. When we interviewed her on January 22, 2018, she said, "There are women who cannot stand what some call paternalism. I think it is something to take advantage of, because it is often an act of kindness. It's more women who have held me back."

I personally never felt any problems related to me being a woman. Is it because I immediately placed myself on equal footing with my partner, who happened to be my husband, or because I did not experience the adventure of being in a large business?

Making your way in large corporations

> *Find the smartest people you can and surround yourself with them.*
> —Marissa Meyer, CEO, Yahoo!

It is not uncommon to encounter gender barriers when building a career in a large company. This was very true 10 or 15 years ago, although less so today. Success depends largely on company culture and your ability to understand male codes, such as competition and hierarchy, without complying with them, and perhaps even managing to play with the model, such as by affirming your uniqueness or willingness to collaborate and putting the group before personal success. Julie-Elya Hasson studied agricultural engineering. She spent ten years working for large corporations, as well as ten years in entrepreneurship, and has held various positions, such as CEO and digital marketing officer, branch manager and international production quality officer. She observed that corporate culture could be more feminine or masculine. At L'Oréal, most of the top executives are men and ideally male characteristics should be shown, but it is less a question of gender than of attitude. Estée Lauder has a very feminine corporate culture, although it is also run by men; it is therefore easier for a woman to advance by staying herself. Retail distribution is very masculine (there is only one woman on Carrefour's board of directors), but e-commerce, where Elya was digital, marketing, customers and innovation director for Carrefour-Rue du Commerce, is one of the most "ungendered" sectors. For her, one model is not better than the other. Often it is the leader who sets the tone. She suggests that women remain focused on their values. With time and professionalism, gender no longer has a role to play. However, there are three strata regularly observed in the large corporations: boards of directors (male—even when the quotas set up in France are reached, the women are most often administrators rather than operational), senior management (mostly male), and middle management and operations (mixed).

Before becoming an entrepreneur in the nutritional coaching sector, Maïa Baudelaire worked for a long time in multinationals like Kellogg's and Unilever. Unilever is a very masculine Anglo-Dutch group. Maïa was in meetings where she had five minutes to vote her budget for an entire region. At a certain job level, women were rare and she was one of the few to have a husband and children, most women having sacrificed their personal lives to their careers. Maïa likes to laugh a lot, and she overcame the tough moments using the absurd to downplay stress, and thanks to women sticking together. To put herself on equal footing with her Dutch male counterparts, who were physically very tall, Maïa wore high heels and never spoke to them while sitting. Sometimes she used stereotypes, playing a hysterical role to get her message across loud and clear. "In both Kellogg's and Unilever, there were always discussions about how to get women into a leadership positions. Men are often predators in business—if a man loves your ideas, he will take them for himself. It takes a certain tenacity to claim them and bring them to fruition," Maïa said in our interview on January 24, 2018. Fortunately, she was also pushed by men who like to work with women—there are some like that.

Isabelle Bordry, who I interviewed on January 26, 2018, began her career at Hachette Filipacchi before joining Yahoo! France in 1997, where she took over as general manager in the early 2000s. During the first period, between 1997 and 2000, Yahoo! was an industry leader. There was no real alternative. Yahoo! was the first media on the Internet and was a reference in the market. "Everything we touched turned to gold. We were creating new models. Advertisers were asking us to build tailor-made solutions. I was meeting with all the media advertising top guns, who wanted to better understand the strategy of this American startup. I never felt slowed down by being a woman until I became executive director. For the first time, I felt I was perceived differently, especially within my teams. For some, it was a double penalty: I was younger than they were, and I was a woman. Sometimes it was hard to get them to accept that."

Turning-point generations

> *If you educate a man you educate one person. If you educate a woman you educate a nation.*
> —African Proverb

With the mention of Yahoo!, I can't help but mention one of the most famous women in tech: Marissa Mayer. At age 37, she became the youngest woman to head a Fortune 500 company. Marissa was very controversial. She has been much heckled in a world of men and criticized both for her presence in women's magazines and for her management style, for her salary equal to a man's and her failure to turn Yahoo! back around, and her decision not to take maternity leave at the birth of her twins. This is not the place to make judgments or try to distinguish between what is true and what is false. Yet, I do not remember seeing any equivalent uprising against a male leader in the same context. I admire Marissa's tenacity standing up for herself and for launching a new project, Lumi Labs.

I am part of this same generation. We are daughters of mothers of who were in their twenties when France's women's liberation movement kickstarted in 1968. Society has sentenced us to succeed in everything, immediately—our relationships, family life, professional life. Yet we still stand in the shadow of a society preferring a female presence at home, but with a real desire for change.

When a young French woman of my generation decided to undertake both family and career, she was still described as "ambitious," even an "upstart"—a powerful critical value judgment.

She was dropped in a box. To change course, a whole generation of women adopted a more masculine attitude in order to be accepted in a society that is still very male-oriented and even misogynist. I'm reminded of the movie Working Girl. The main character is a secretary whose boss steals her idea and she steals it back by pretending she had her boss's job.

Women cannot and should not behave like men. At a conference I attended in May 2017, Hillary Clinton noted that she could not use the same rhetorical techniques as men. It was impossible for a female politician to harangue the crowd or to anger without being labeled hysterical.

Odile Roujol, interviewed on November 27, 2017, worked in the beauty industry for twenty years, including thirteen at L'Oréal corporate. At 37, she became the youngest CEO of Lancôme, one of the three largest global brands in the group, leader in selective cosmetics, present in 135 countries. At 41, she chose to change industries and to discover the constantly changing world of tech and data. She spent six years at the Telecom corporation Orange, first as director of communications and then chief strategy and data officer. I met her in San Francisco, where she had been living for two years and had started a third life, advising startup CEOs and venture capitalists.

"Like most of L'Oréal's top managers, I was considered an 'assertive' leader, with a style that, in hindsight, was quite masculine —quick to make decisions, results oriented," Odile said. "On the other hand, I think I also had a fairly feminine approach, always fighting for my teams in the infamous talent reviews. However, I admit it took me a long time to realize the importance of people. Orange was an industry leader, dominant on the French market, but the company had just experienced a major social crisis when I joined it in 2009. A difficult economic context followed with the arrival of a new low-cost entrant (Free, with billionaire businessman Xavier Niel at the head). This led me to think more about the impact I had on others, about the content of my messages, and about my role as manager. L'Oréal was a pool of multicultural talents, more business oriented, with highly qualified people. Orange was a technology-driven, analytical, process-oriented, risk-weighting company, with technical experts and a majority of engineers, most of whom had a career in the company, some with government worker status. Being on the executive committee of a company with more than 80,000 employees in the French market alone makes you think about what message you communicate and how teams participate. In short, I learned about collective intelligence, and that we could build a strategy with people close to customers and the field."

Today, Odile mentors many entrepreneurs and speaks at conferences on leadership, governance, and the role of boards. She is spreading the message, "People first." She has also just created the Beauty Tech Community (www.beautytechcommunity.com).

Alice Guilhon, a former academic and an expert in economic intelligence at the French Ministry of the Interior, is now the dean of my former business school, SKEMA. During our interview on March 13, 2018, she perfectly summed up the persistence of success and gender stereotypes: "When I made powerful decisions, I was always surprised to hear people say 'That lady's got some balls,' meaning that if I succeeded, I was behaving like a man. If you are tough and you manage like a man, then you succeed— it's stupid."

Men are not our role models, and we are not here to take anybody's place. We have a place of our own, but we only claimed it belatedly. Women have long remained behind the scenes. How many times have we heard that "behind every great man there is a woman"? Today, all this is coming to the surface, and the importance of women is bursting forth. For my part, I deeply admire woman like Simone Veil. This great lady defended women from deepest part of herself, and she was a role model who succeeded in all of her lives, all her missions—daughter, mother, wife, woman of power, without forgetting her career. Christine Lagarde is also a woman who inspires me enormously. She's probably my role model in business, and I'm lucky to know her a little bit. She has succeeded in keeping a very human side, very anchored in reality despite her position.

I had the opportunity to meet Christine Lagarde for the first time in Davos at the World Economic Forum, while she was working in Foreign Trade. At the time, my ex-husband was doing a lot of podcasts and she dabbled in this new interview format. I was immediately inspired by her elegance and ease of access. Two years later, when she was Minister of the Economy, we invited her to take part in the awards ceremony of our startup competition at LeWeb, which was the first event to bring all of Silicon Valley's key players to Paris. Her responsibilities made for an extremely busy schedule. We made a direct request to her, and I think her advisors did everything they could to dissuade her from accepting. Not only did she answer our request for an interview, she also stayed throughout the startup presentations, taking the time to listen to them all. At the time, one of her sons was launching a startup, and she made this nice comment to the entrepreneurs who participated: "Thank you. I understand better now what my son is doing."

Role models are paramount for mentalities to change. In 2012, MIT economist Esther Duflo published a study demonstrating the importance of role models. The more we are in the presence of women who have managed to combine everything and succeed smoothly, the more we can overcome what is slowing us down.

At the École nationale d'administration, which is considered France's top academic institution that trains senior French officials and government ministers, Fleur Pellerin was part of the most mixed class the school has seen since it was founded (about 35% of women). During her studies, she did not feel at all discriminated against because of her appearance, Asian background, or her gender. This is the advantage of the competition-based merit system, which is very egalitarian. But once in public service, she found that the directors of the central administrations were always men, and she saw how difficult it could be to change things. For her, it is the education of children and the messages sent to them that will change the situation. "My 13-year-old daughter saw me in positions of responsibility. It will be much less complex to have equal status within the couple, to ask for the same salary as a man. She can easily imagine herself in such circumstances. Between the ages of seven and twelve years, she almost never saw me. It was not easy, but she does not blame me. I think that if she faces this type of choice later, it will be without feeling the guilt felt by the generation of our mothers or even ours. I never really talked to her, but she understood why I made that choice, she was proud of her mom. We are a blended family, so really the modern family par excellence. At one point, her stepfather was a chief of staff in a government ministry, so we had a very crazy family life. She understood that we were discussing how to balance things. When I was appointed to foreign trade, I was always on airplanes, and my husband joined the public service. He made that choice because we felt it was better for her. Today, there are many more men who agree to question themselves than there were fifteen years ago, more who question the predominance of men in providing income, the couple's career status, etc. I try to make sure that my daughter does not close any horizon. She has a passion for space, she did her third internship at the European Space Agency. It is very important to help girls to project themselves into a world of engineers and research that remains very masculine."

It is very important for Fleur to be an example for her daughter. She had to free herself from the model of her own mother, who was very available to her children because she was a housewife. Because of this model, she has sometimes had to struggle with the idea that the quality of education is very much related to the amount of time spent with children. Spending a lot of time at work causes women to feel more guilt than it does men. There is a collective intelligence of the family that, depending on the period, the father or mother can balance his or her presence with the children, but we are not yet free from the model where a woman follows her spouse. Similarly, as Delphine Bellini, General Manager of the Schiaparelli couture house, commented, "Spousal support is very important for women. This makes them quieter and more sure of themselves. This support reassures them that the family balance will not be shaken in difficult times. Two people are always stronger."

Inventing a new standard

You have to hold on to the opportunity of being a woman, to be a Swiss knife where men are just knives. Starting a business does not mean becoming a bulldozer overnight.
—Hélène Duval, founder of YUJ

We are not here to build a new active-woman stereotype. We are in the age of the personalized and on-demand rather than ready-to-wear that should suit everyone. It's time to refuse molds in order to create our own shape, to redraw the lines. Old models are falling to pieces. How can we be part of this change?

Let's keep our identity as women, rather than melt into the codes of the existing system to achieve a success that would not resemble us. Certainly, in some ways, women must learn from men, and we cannot be completely free from comparison. But as women, we start with excellent foundations. Men and women should seek to inspire each other. Men, for example, could be inspired by a form of finesse found in women who tend to gather all the pieces before acting. They could also learn to give us a little more space, to appreciate that we can juggle different subjects and activities better than they can. Everything starts from trust. It is by being mature in our approach that we will achieve a symbiosis; but this is hard work that takes time. We must encourage all initiatives that can enable women to develop projects and careers, because the problem we face is that we must potentially combine not one, but three careers, that of mother, that of companion and that of professional. Do not choose!

Digital technology has redrawn the lines by allowing the rise of microenterprises created by women. On the Etsy platform, created in 2005, 87 percent of sellers are women and 40 percent of them had never marketed their creations before doing it online. This is a superb illustration of the range of possibilities opened up by new technologies. The traditional model of success no longer holds. Having a career no longer means anything to the younger generations. With the gig economy in full swing, Lyft and Uber being prime examples, we can no longer imagine linear trajectories. Some people do not even want to have a permanent contract, favoring freelance activities. This shift could become an unprecedented opportunity for women, allowing them to invent a new way of working, one more in harmony with their balance. For those who choose to start a family, why not imagine a career path with several phases aligned with the children's growth? Millennials are very attentive to controlling their identity at work, and they have less desire to blend in with company requirements than to become "egopreneurs," to use the term coined by Jean-Louis Magakian, professor in strategy and organization at EMLyon Business School. "At a time when everyone is seen as replaceable, investing in oneself makes it possible to make oneself indispensable to oneself."

I met Marion Moreau at the time of LeWeb. She was a journalist for FrenchWeb. On a side note, since 2016, we have both been part of a French Tech entrepreneurs' non-profit band that plays to highlight initiatives supporting entrepreneurship. That said, above all, Marion's career path provides a very good example of imaginative reinvention. At 19, she studied at the Sorbonne and dreamed about becoming a journalist. To finance her studies, she started looking for odd jobs and ended up at Club Internet, one of the first French Internet providers. The company decided to set up a content portal, and she became the first print journalist to work online. Throughout her career, Marion has always remained in this dynamic, very close to what we now call "innovation." Subsequently, as a freelancer, she spent five years developing FrenchWeb alongside Richard Menneveux, one of her former colleagues at Club Internet. It was then that she crossed paths with Ludovic Le Moan, the founder of Sigfox, who had a business project and suggested she take the lead. He gave her carte blanche. It was a big challenge, as she had never done anything similar. When we interviewed her on October 10, 2017, she had been working on this large-scale project for two years with the goal of putting the Internet of Things to work for humanitarian aid. "My biggest challenge has been getting out of the way," she said. "I was slightly dizzy when I left my job. The nature of what I have been asked to do was extraordinary. Being free was scary, but it was a great opportunity to be at the heart of a new project. I'm interested in technology and in meaning. I'm surrounded by nothing but engineers. It's so rewarding to come across catalysts, to work with explorers, people who make discoveries. There is a lot of energy and luck involved. The foundation is still very small. It is a heavy burden to carry, but we will get there." Marion started with a project in Antarctica following the suggestion of a Belgian startup founder. Curiosity drove her. She invites everyone to try their luck.

"Every man and every woman has creativity inside. You have to look for and find your north star. Jean-Louis Étienne only had a milling turner's certificate before becoming the first man to reach the North Pole. Everything is possible if you want it to be, there are no barriers. I would like girls the age of my daughter, who is 11 years old, to say, 'If you think it's a good idea and it makes a contribution, you have to fight for it.' You have to consider a project not as a possible option, but as a true conviction. There is a place for all women who have a wish, a desire, a little flame just waiting to kindle. Whether you are driven to open a decoration shop or want to rub shoulders with the big shots of the world, the challenge is worth it. There are many women whose ambition is asleep. For me, life is a passage and as it is a passage, there is no time to lose. My hope is that women experience work as a love story. Fortunately, we are moving towards that, towards work environments that combine know-how, well-being, and fulfillment."

Marion's daily challenge includes her two children. "They are my mission, I place them before everything else, although not always in my daily life. But I organized a life that allows us to experience powerful moments together. I do not hear many women in tech talking about family, when that is our balance. There is a place for women entrepreneurs who are also moms. I hope we are showing our daughters, and our sons, that there is not just one model."

Tomorrow, women's journeys will not be standardized, and I hope that the multiplicity of testimonials gathered in this book will give you an idea of the scope of what is already possible today. But if there is one point on which all the women I interviewed agree, it is the importance of financial independence. "Independence is the crux of it all," says Sibylle de Villeneuve, the founder of the media relations agency Raoul in an interview on January 24, 2018. "I have three sisters who have had a good education, but none of them worked. It changes a lifetime. I would not change mine for all the gold in the world. I paid the high price, but today my freedom is priceless. I say it almost every day."

Others echo what she says. "My mother always insisted on how important financial independence is to women, as it allows them to make their own choices. That was probably the best advice that I ever received," Corinne Vigreux said. Maïa Baudelaire's mother also gave her two common sense pieces of advice when she was young: "Always stay independent, even as a married woman—never depend on a man. And don't be in any hurry to marry." This advice remained anchored in her mind—she needed to be herself above all else.

Clementine Piazza, founder of InMemori says the same. "We must not give up financial independence at any price. To create it makes it possible to build, to make choices, and to leave when necessary. My father told me when I was a kid, 'We work so we can always feed ourselves, keep warm, and not depend on anyone.' I was lucky enough to be told that soon enough." If there is a new standard to invent, it is a model that allows all women this freedom.

In praise of diversity

I do not want to rank among women, I want to rank among everyone.
—Rania Belkahia, co-founder of Afrimarket

Sibylle de Villeneuve introduced me to Myriam Maestroni, the founder of Economie d'Energie, whom she met at Stanford in an entrepreneurial program initiated by Martine Liautaud, founder of the Women Initiative Foundation. Myriam has spent most of her career in a very male sector (the oil industry) and believes that women will save the world. "I was lucky in my life, I found remarkable men; those who are a little less remarkable are terrified of women who can save the world. Unfortunately, there is a resurgence of this kind of behavior. Women have a sense for managing many parameters simultaneously, while masculine energy is focused, going from the problem to the solution. To save the world, we must understand that it is all important, from the quality of relationships to money, children, and order. The latter manifests from harmony. Female energy is a complete energy that touches many things at the same time. Our way of life is better adapted to a complex world where we can no longer operate by iteration. There are plenty of men who do not want to discuss things and who attack not your ideas, but you. For women to save the world, we need to ensure that men who cannot understand let the women do what they have to do."

What posture should a woman adopt in a man's universe? An egalitarian stance. The question is not "Am I a man or a woman?" but, "What do I bring as a person to my company, my professional world, etc.?" I would not want to found a business in which there were only women, it would not be balanced. Single-sex schools have had their day; in companies too, the mix of teams in terms of gender, age, experience, and culture is crucial.

David Gurlé, the founder of Symphony (a startup specializing in encrypted messages), managed to hire 50 percent women in his highly technological company. This is the result of a deliberate choice based on the belief that diversity is the foundation of success and that women often have a very different approach to solutions. This means giving the employees the means to perform their role of mother—the company grants six months of maternity leave (which is not common in the United States) and arranges schedules so parents can work from wherever they want.

Since the first 2015 publication of Why Diversity Matters, McKinsey & Company has seen a growing awareness of the importance of inclusion and diversity in business. The report made a lot of noise and largely influenced the balancing measures taken in private and public sector enterprises and in NGOs around the world. The first motivation has obviously been to meet legal obligations, but many successful companies see diversity as a competitive advantage and a growth accelerator. In January 2018, the consulting firm published a second research component, Delivering Through Diversity. It defines diversity as the presence of a large proportion of women and people from ethnically and culturally diverse backgrounds and reaffirms the correlation between diversity in the leadership of large companies and financial outperformance. The study concerns a sample of more than 1,000 companies in 12 countries. The report demonstrates a persistent correlation between leadership diversity and economic performance. Top quartile companies in terms of gender diversity in management teams had a 21 percent chance of outperforming in profitability and an additional 27 percent chance in creating value. The most successful companies had more women in key roles. It's not just about gender: top-quartile companies in terms of ethnic and cultural diversity of executive teams were 33 percent more likely to be leaders in their sector in profitability. This suggests that broad diversity in all respects (age, international experience, etc.) can be key to differentiation. Conversely, the bad students are penalized. Across the panel, last-quartile firms for both gender and ethnic and cultural diversity are 29 percent less likely to have a higher return than average. To sum things up, not only are they not leaders, but they are lagging behind. Australian, American, and British companies perform best in terms of gender diversity. For ethnic diversity, South African and Singaporean firms rate highest.

More diverse companies are more likely to attract the best talent, listen to their customers, satisfy their employees, and make good decisions. Correlation does not mean cause, but the significant statistical relationship between wide-scale diversity in management teams of large companies and financial performance can be a real incentive to redraw the lines.

The McKinsey report cites among its champions of gender diversity the case of Sodexo, a French multinational whose board of directors is chaired by a woman, Sophie Bellon. The group is publicly committed to promoting five dimensions of diversity: gender, disability, generations, cultures and origins, and sexual orientation. Achieving parity was the starting point. The company's internal research revealed that better representation of women (between 40 and 60 percent) in management positions was correlated with higher performance on aspects such as customer satisfaction and employee involvement. The company is committed to reaching 40 percent women senior executives by 2025. Management is encouraged to achieve these parity goals through concrete rewards, such as a 10 percent bonus. Effort pays. Today women represent 50 percent of the board of directors, 32 percent of senior executives and nearly 50 percent of the overall workforce. Sodexo is one of the most mixed companies in its sector (and in France). It is also one of the most financially successful companies according to the McKinsey panel, with value creation at 13 percent above the sector average.

Even in a tiny startup, one can look for diverse profiles. Clémentine Piazza did just that at InMemori, bringing together a team of six multicultural people from different ethnic backgrounds.

Diversity calls forth talent. Men must understand this and overcome their fear of working with women. Gender diversity must be promoted first and foremost in schools and universities in order to be able to flow naturally to companies, and so that the paradigm of the respective places of women and men will change at last. I spoke at a roundtable one day with Ravleen Beeston, Microsoft London's sales director, who said that her male colleagues were perfectly happy to take their children to the dentist at 5 p.m.

Among Leetchi and Mangopay's 95 or so team members, there are many new fathers who are very involved in their fatherhood. In 2017, the company increased paternity leave to three weeks for all its offices. "If we, who have a company DNA so open to diversity, do not move the lines, who will?" asks Céline Lazorthes. The corporate social responsibility manager of its shareholder, Crédit Mutuel Arkéa, drew her attention to the fact that in order to promote gender equality, meetings should not be organized after 6 p.m. The details of organization matter. Céline has made sure that there is maximum flexibility in the company's rules, as long as it is for the good of all.

In the world of investors, venture capitalists tend to seek female associates. It is still a man's world, but women have a lot to offer, starting with a vision, a different way of approaching problems. It is this collective intelligence that must be brought into artificial intelligence. Today, a school like Epitech, one of the leading schools of engineering in France, which trains the best developers of tomorrow, has less than four percent women. Among them is Dipty Chander (@diptychander on Twitter), who is initiating many projects to change this unbalance. Artificial intelligence algorithms that will condition our future society are being created on the basis of a male point of view and we should not let this happen. The world of technology is fallow: there is a place for women to take. It's now or never and I'm glad to see many initiatives both in the United States and in France to make it happen. Note that if women are not yet sufficiently involved in the design of algorithms, it is always feminized robots that we choose to embody the virtual assistants, be it Apple's Siri, Amazon's Alexa, Microsoft's Cortana, or more recently, Erica from Bank of America. Long live programs that do not contribute to maintaining gender stereotypes.

It is also important to increase the proportion of women in the investment sector. On one hand, if obstacles keep women from this labor market, the sector loses a pool of talent. On the other hand, inequality itself can be harmful because limiting points of view limits possibilities. Assumptions suggest that women's decision-making characteristics differ from those of men, a subject widely debated regarding women's participation in boards of directors.

An expert in business turnaround, Helen Bouygues thinks that more women should do the work she does. "I think I'm more analytical than men in the context of crisis management," she said when we interviewed her on October 11, 2017. "It's a requirement as a woman. Unlike men, my ego is irrelevant." She now focuses on critical thinking with her new venture Reboot Foundation, an organization that aims to better integrate critical thinking into the daily lives of people around the world.

I interviewed Isabelle Bordry on January 26, 2018. She has managed many teams throughout her career and, without going into stereotypes, she has observed differences in behavior—women are generally more studious than men, with a real ability to stick to tight schedules, while men are often excellent in sales and motivated by the competition. She also notes that women have more freedom from their professional careers and fewer social pressures than men, especially financially, which gives them much more freedom in their choices and perhaps less fear of failure. "At the end of my university education, after studying finance and management, unlike the large majority of my classmates, I chose to work in media rather than auditing or finance. I never acted by making career plans, but by following my desires, never saying to myself that I had to build a career under financial pressure from my entourage. If I had been a man, I would have probably made different choices. Whenever I can, I defend women's rights and the principles of equal representation. Differences in pay for equal work are, for me, one of the great injustices against which we still have to struggle. I think equal pay comes hand in hand with a real change in attitudes towards men, with a desire to let go of the career pressure society places on men—not looking at them any differently if they push a stroller one afternoon a week or if they leave their work hastily because their child is sick. We still have a lot to learn from the Scandinavian countries."

For Frédérique Dame, being a woman is a strength. "I have qualities that a man does not have. I will put forward those qualities that are so unique to me and that define my type of leadership. I have always refused to compete with men over their strengths." Being different is an exceptional opportunity to venture out of the mold. Frédérique also finds it important to have a very diversified network. Your next big opportunity may come to you from someone you met at the sports club or while volunteering.

Founder of the OneRagtime investment fund, Stéphanie Hospital served as Executive Vice President of Orange Digital. Orange is a leading telecom company that has always been open to diversity, supporting and encouraging. Stéphanie has kept this openness and has transposed it in the OneRagtime team, rich in a wide variety of ages, genders, and cultures.

When she started presenting her plan to set up a fund, Stephanie went to see a head of the European Investment Fund who thought she would launch a fund to finance women's projects. This reaction surprised her; what she wanted was to finance good projects, by men or women. "It's not because I'm a woman that I'm going to fund women's projects and do a digital manicure bar. In projects undertaken by women entrepreneurs, there are often very feminine projects. We tell them, 'If it's a passion, go ahead, but if you can come up with a very innovative project in artificial intelligence, it's even better.'"

During her career, Stéphanie was mostly supported by men. If we want more women in the sectors that lack them, the support of both men and women will be crucial. "If there is a mission that should be given to women activists, it is to put forward men who understand women, who play the game of true diversity without the dogma, those who don't wait for quotas to bring women on to their board of directors," says Marion Moreau, director of the Sigfox Foundation. "Behind a woman there is always a man!"

Chapter 2
Safeguarding Personal Fulfillment

My life did not please me, so I created my life.
—Coco Chanel

I have always put my family first. This balance brings me happiness. It's related to my character, but perhaps also to my education, because I belong to a transition generation. I did not plan to prioritize my own development, particularly in terms of my career. I wanted to do everything. At 23, already married and mother to my oldest son, Arthur, I felt I was prepared to focus fully on my career with the certainty that I would not be asked the question, "Will you want children?" I was going to build my career with two boxes already checked off: married, mother.

I was determined to chart my career path, but I had not yet considered starting my own business. It must be said that in 1995, nobody was talking about startups, let alone financing. Imagine a world that was just discovering the Internet.

In 1994, my now-former husband, Loïc Le Meur, had invested our modest savings in the purchase of a PC with a modem, pieced together by an assembler in the streets of old Nice. We were settled in Antibes and he was spending a gap year at Texas Instruments in Villeneuve-Loubet. There we were with a machine that filled the table in the middle of our only room. The modem popping out its "beep ... beep bip bip," our connections to Compuserve and Yahoo! stammering, on a green-on-black screen with what one could barely call definition. But it was a whole new world that was opening up. I know how unlikely it seems today, but I remember the excitement when we used Compuserve to book a hotel in Italy to celebrate our first wedding anniversary! Internet was entering our lives.

In my third year of studies at SKEMA Business School, it is a woman who closed the first door on me when I was doing my required internship. Arthur would be born in August 1995, and this was mid-April. On my first day of the internship, I landed in the beautiful Parisian offices of a large luxury group, in the eighth arrondissement. My internship manager told me that I had to go for the compulsory medical examination with the occupational doctor. For her, as for me, it was a formality. I walked the 800 meters that separated me from the occupational health center on the Champs-Elysees. I climbed up the stairs and a few minutes later, the doctor saw me. I felt confident, she was a woman. And then, everything fell apart. Seeing my pretty round belly, she spouted off a verbal diatribe, offended that the large corporation in question was "exploiting trainees, and pregnant ones at that." She did not even examine me. She didn't listen to any of my arguments, handing me a document refusing me the right to do my internship. I was back to square one. I was supposed to put everything on hold to have my kid. I had a hard time accepting that prospect. How could a woman do this to me?

My second disappointment came soon enough after Arthur's birth. This time, I no longer had a big belly, so there wouldn't be any risk. In October 1995, I managed to find a spot in a nursery and responded to a job offer from a media agency that was looking for people to join its brand new interactive team. Bingo! After two interviews, I landed my first (and last) position: project manager on a fixed-term contract in the agency's interactive unit. Sure of my well-oiled organization and my working abilities, I deposited Arthur at daycare at 7:45 a.m., arrived at 8:30 at the latest at the office in Levallois-Perret, worked full-time all day long (I didn't spend much time at the coffee machine) and, at 6:15 p.m. at the latest, I would run off to get Arthur at the nursery (we didn't have the means for a babysitter). Woe is me! How could I even consider not hanging out at the office until 8 p.m.? It was as if I had taken the afternoon off. In short, there was no prospect of fulfillment in this system, and above all there was tremendous frustration, a feeling of injustice that revolted me a little more every day.

When I was pregnant with Gauthier my second son, his father and I were both working in our first company, B2L, and at the time I was working under my maiden name. The business was small, and we were young, so to call us "Mr. and Mrs." sounded a little odd. Our customers did not know that we were married. One day, a customer said to Loïc, "Your project manager looks really pregnant. She's not going to drop us in the middle, is she?" He answered, "No, it's fine. I'm confident." I was lucky because my older children were born in the summer, Arthur in August and Gauthier in June, which was easier for "maternity leave." But that wasn't the question for me. My life was organized around my children and my companies.

In September 1997, I created my second company, RapidSite France (web hosting), just in time for Gauthier's arrival. I had no intention of being overwhelmed by guilt and had made the choice to lead my two lives, mother and entrepreneur, in my own way. So, I put together a team of about ten people to surround me and everyone knew that starting at 6:30 p.m., I was no longer there. I was in mom mode for three hours every day. I went home, bathed the kids, cooked dinner, spent time doing the bedtime ritual, and around 9 p.m., I was available again to handle emergencies. I remember that my ex-husband had a lot of doubts: "Who knows what will happen if you're out of there at 6 p.m." No, this was not a "when the cat is away the mice will play" model. It was just a different mode of operation that I applied to myself and to my teams.

At the time of LeWeb, I worked a lot at home. One day, my youngest son, Grégoire, who is now 17 years old and who lived through the LeWeb period as a child, told me: "You were working like crazy." He felt that if I had not been home, it would be the same because when I was behind my desk, I did not want to be disturbed. From the moment you have a business, you are bound to it body and soul. I think that's important.

Through entrepreneurship, despite the challenges, I found the possibility to have a family without anyone dictating or imposing choices on me. I am convinced that everything plays out in the early years and often results from a sum of tiny details put end to end in the simple acts of everyday life. All the moments are important. When the children were small, I dreaded moving to the United States, because my organization was extremely well oiled in Paris, with important practical details in place, such as renting my offices near the school. In the United States, I was afraid of being a little stuck in a system where I knew very well that support for early childhood was not the same. I never had a full-time nanny (anyway, when I had my children, I did not have the means to have one). I was afraid I would not be able to continue. In 2007, my eldest son finished sixth grade and we said to ourselves, "If we don't go now, we won't go." Arthur was entering adolescence, he was 12 years old. After that, it would have been too late and this desire to go to the heart of the Internet reactor, in San Francisco, was extremely present. So, we did it.

Since 2007, I have been based in San Francisco. When I moved into the Valley, I did not expect so many cultural differences. My first networking experiences were complicated to say the least. As I had chosen to be with my husband in an entrepreneurial adventure that we had built together, his story was mine and vice versa. In truth, it was not so vice versa. Our story remained mostly his. As I had three boys, by default, it was assumed that I was taking care of my children full time. I suffered at the beginning because I was only asked questions about the kids with the ulterior motive that since I "worked" with my husband, it meant he could not afford to support his family and that I did not have to look far to find a "job" to keep me busy.

Now that my children are grown up, a decade later, a reverse phenomenon is happening. My oldest son already has a US degree in his pocket and took his first position at Google, my second is about to graduate and will go to Google too, also in the United States, and the last will leave the nest in June 2019 to go to Princeton. So, my rather atypical profile has become an opportunity. I am 46 years old, and I have full professional freedom of choice and movement.

I knew that my children were going to leave at some point, that they did not belong to me. I wanted to build around them, but not for them alone. It is important to develop yourself as well. Children are my priority, the center of gravity of my life, but we cannot sacrifice for them. Moreover, it would not help them because I think that what they see from us on a daily basis is also very important—a child will follow your example, and much more rarely your advice. The path I have taken since the age of 23 reconciled my own development and that of my children. We are here to put children on a path. The years they are at home are a passage in their lives, the moment they build their foundations. My "youngest" will take flight, but my life will continue. That will not stop at his departure. For 23 years, my daily life has been organized around my children, they punctuated it, but this period will end (even if, of course, they remain ubiquitous), and today is a new stage in my life.

If a woman wants to have children and she doesn't, she will not be able to fully engage herself professionally. I have also always been convinced that children are sponges. Whatever the situation, a fulfilled mother has well-rounded children. For me, it's balance that counts; the moment we find it, we can do everything. It does not really make sense to create a dichotomy between professional and personal—life is a whole.

Does maternity have to be an obstacle?

> *Being a woman entrepreneur is the ultimate expression of freedom.*
> —Caroline Ramade

If there is one thing that belongs only to women, it is maternity. The latter is often perceived as an obstacle, with the underlying idea that we cannot do everything well. For me, the power to give life is an undisputed force that women have, a form of power that no one can take away from us. I am not saying that being a mother is an absolute goal, just that it is in our DNA, that we are built that way. We are creative—entrepreneurial by nature.

In France, we are doing fairly well. At least, the system allows women to put children in childcare, where in Germany, for example, the idea that a woman has to stop working to devote herself to the education of the children remains very much alive. The school system selects children from the age of seven, and there is strong social pressure on the mothers regarding their children's success, doing homework with them, and getting them into the best possible school. As a result, in Germany, 49 percent of women in managerial and executive positions are single and without children, according to Annie Combelles, who we interviewed on March 8, 2018. Similarly, the United States is one of only three countries in the world that has no maternity leave. The American school system also requires a great deal of time from parents and, for the moment, women undertake 60 to 70 percent of educational tasks. Some women succeed by giving up their family life.

The idea of choosing between professional success and raising a family is hard to change and continues to widen the gender gap. "Our biological clock is an inequality," says Stéphanie Hospital. "It's a difficult factor in male-female relationships. This temporal barrier is a fundamental difference between men and women. But there are women who show that it is possible."

In the United States, companies like Google and Apple are trying to respond to worries expressed by young women who want a career and are afraid that one day their biological clock will strike with a cruel reminder of its limits. The solution these companies are proposing is an offer to freeze the women's eggs, which is very expensive (this can be counted in thousands or tens of thousands of dollars). For me, this proposal is typical of a man's response to a woman's problem. It offers the illusion of control over one's life and empowerment, without solving the real issues. Not to mention that, despite advances in medicine, there is no full guarantee of having children from frozen eggs. On average, a 36-year-old woman who freezes 10 eggs has a 30 to 60 percent chance of having a child using them.

My vision is more in line with that of Caroline Ramade. For her, women entrepreneurs will change the world because they take responsibility for their family and consider that all humanity should do the same. Women can lead to a new distribution of tasks, but not if they give up and accept to succeed as men have done so far, leaving family life aside. We must invent success that does not involve sacrificing family life. After generations of men never considering the question, they will have to share the intimate sphere. A balanced world will be one where women can focus on work, as can men, and where men can also focus on their families, alongside women.

I also believe we need to help women think ahead, and I support initiatives such as Modernfertility.com. I met the founder Afton Vechery at The Lobby conference, and her approach to help raise young women's awareness is definitely a right move.

Being a mother in the corporate world

I don't like the word 'businesswoman.' Perhaps 'committed mother' would be the best description.

—Steffi Graf

Odile Roujol has two grown sons who are now students in Canada. She did not choose to push back the birth of her children to make room for her career, as she sees young women in Silicon Valley doing today. When she was at the helm of Lancôme, she spent a lot of time on planes, unsurprisingly, since the brand's biggest market was the United States and more than 20 percent of sales in Asia. She was also sent to New York on a two-year assignment, leaving with husband and children in the middle of the school year.

Travel sometimes takes place on Sunday, so you can be ready to start on Monday morning, which is a real challenge when you have two children. This hectic pace is also a challenge for couples, as Odile experienced. "We frequently had family meetings to weigh options for my spouse or for me. We had to find a pace where we were both inspired by our work and yet had the impression to succeeding our life. Time is a very precious resource. I felt like it was slipping through my fingers. In the corporate world, your schedule depends a lot on others, and it started to weigh on me. I was a bit of a caricature of 1990's wonder woman. I remember attending a business review meeting with Lindsay Owen-Jones in New York. Oscar, my son, was six years old. He had told me the day before: 'For two days my friends have shared their lunch with me.' That morning, I left for the office and realized that I had forgotten his meal again. I run back home, brought the lunchbox to school, and arrived at the meeting disheveled, barely catching my breath, two minutes before Owen-Jones entered the room. My division boss turned to me, surprised and a little snarky, and said, 'Odile, what happened to you?' In that moment, I felt great solitude, and said it with a smile that I was unable to explain, we were too different in our daily life and in our priorities."

"We always feel guilty," she continued. "Many of my sons' schoolmates' mothers dedicating their lives to their children. My sons, who are now 20 and 22 years old, reassured me laughing, 'You have so much energy, mom, that it would have been a nightmare to have you at home! You raised us to be independent and find our way, that's what good parents do.' I feel like I did that, but it's easy to say so afterwards. I like the African proverb that says, 'It takes a village to raise a child.'"

For Odile, you need to have a circle of trust around you to be good at what you do and to succeed. "Everyone invents their own rules of the game. I was fortunate to be supported by my mother, by my husband, who happily at the time was traveling less than I was, and super nannies who my children continue to see and who contributed to their education and their values. They saw their Filipino nanny educate her children at a distance, relying on the solidarity of her family, and being a model of courage and good humor. My sons are respectful of different cultures and of each person's work. I was fortunate to have opportunities in my career and to seize them without the impression of sacrificing my family life."

Isabelle Bordry belongs to the same pivotal generation as Odile and me. Her personal experience as a woman who, in her first life, had a good career as a salaried employee, is that you have more freedom for children when you hold a leadership position. When she had her children, she was the CEO of Yahoo! France, which did not prevent her husband (who worked in finance) to tell her that if one day it was necessary to take the children to the pediatrician, she would be the one to go. "Men, especially in finance, are still subject to strong social pressure. This impacts the agendas of an organization; meetings at 7 p.m. are not possible with children. Multimedia tools and the gift of ubiquity that goes with them have helped a lot. With the BlackBerry, we could answer emails anywhere. This allowed me to think I could succeed. It never crossed my mind to stop work and, like some close friends, transform into a housewife. It even worried me. I never stopped. I remember being eight or nine months' pregnant discussing the launch of new projects with investors. I do not see myself as a full-time mother, and even think I am a good mother because I have professional occupations that are essential to my balance. My mother always blamed me for working. For her, a woman's role was to stay at home. I had been working for 13 or 14 years when I had children and it did not occur to me to stop."

It should be noted that Isabelle was behind the concept of digital mums, which advertisers grabbed onto ten years ago to refer to housewives under 50 years of age. In 2007, ADSL arrived in homes making having Internet as simple as having television. Consumer brands became mainstream online, welcomed by women with a certain euphoria, for online shopping. Isabelle studied women on the Internet, and this change in how they were consuming and discussing everyday life meant that, at the birth of a child, the reflex became to seek answers to questions on blogs rather than calling one's mother. Digital mums inquire and discuss with girlfriends and with brands. Isabelle's idea was to change the vision of women as consumers in a positive way and was taken to task for it by an editorialist of Elle: "Once again we have advertisers who see women as mothers first and foremost." Isabelle had not thought about that for a second, because for her, being a mother is not negative at all and has nothing stigmatizing about it.

When we interviewed Julie-Elya Hasson in December 2017, she had a near end-of-term round belly. She was well placed to share her experience. Working in a large corporation while pregnant is not easy. Especially when she made the brave choice to be a solo mother. "I found myself five months pregnant in meetings where I sat for 11 hours straight. In France, meetings generally last a really long time. With my teams, the important meetings last one hour and a half maximum, and those on the pending subjects, half an hour." This is one of the cultural changes in her profession that she brought back from her years of experience in Silicon Valley. Moreover, medically assisted procreation with sperm from an unknown father had not yet become culturally ordinary in France, whereas in Northern Europe countries, up to 20 percent of births come from this mode of conception. It required courage and resilience to undertake the process and even more to answer questions about it in her environment.

"I live with a slight advance on the times," Julie-Elya explained. "To give life and to give birth to one's child is a miracle, even and especially through medically assisted procreation. The process and hopes are so intense! I know that all those who go through the process need courage and tenacity. I admire any woman who conceives the child of an unknown father and is a single mother, because I know what it takes. I help them and support them as much as I can. It takes resilience to experience it with joy. Life paths are sometimes built in happy chaos—we start with a child and we end up as a couple in blended families. When I went on maternity leave, I wanted things to go as smoothly as possible, so I made an ultra-detailed plan for all my teams with a roadmap for six months and a strategy for 18 months. As a result, everything went well, and I stayed in regular contact, available to support our managers."

Some companies make life easier for mothers, but we are still far from a generalization. Carrefour has a company nursery; Living Lab opened a kindergarten. We are still at the very beginning of integrating different generations. Childcare structures don't have enough spaces to cover needs. More than an evolution, there has to be a real revolution to support new mothers who are going to be more and more often single. We need to start with adjusting working methods. Because women are ambitious and want to safeguard their children's education. "I think it's possible to have a career and a family life, with four children, to have a position of broad responsibility and to be a caring woman," said Julie-Elya. "Françoise Mercadal-Delassales [General Manager of the French bank Crédit du Nord since May 2018] inspires me on a daily basis. She is a model of success, and someone who is personally fabulous."

Annie Combelles was lucky enough to have easy pregnancies for which she had very little need to take time off work. "My second child arrived a little earlier than planned. I was in a pre-certification meeting. Feeling contractions come on, I cut the meeting short and gave birth the same evening. I proposed to finish the meeting at the maternity ward, and the midwife saw five men file in. We had planned for the birth to take place during the holidays because it would allow me time to rest a little more. My grandmother was a farmer and she had her kids in the fields. Pregnancy did not stop her from going to work. It's not an illness. When you have the will to do it, you can do it." Once her children were born, she lived a few tense moments until she found a helper who then stayed in the family for 22 years, leaving in the evening when one of the two parents came home. Annie regularly works at SupAéro, her former school, which remains very strongly male (there are about 40 women out of three classes of 150 students). She is somewhat demoralized to see the same questions arising about the possibility of reconciling professional and personal life. Her generation fought for this, but the answers are not yet clear.

In the two corporations in which Maïa Baudelaire held senior positions, Kellogg's and Unilever, she saw many women end their careers as they raised their children. The ecosystem did not allow them to survive. The only place she saw teams almost 100 percent female was in Brazil, where there was a nursery in the company. It's the best of both worlds, but this case is unfortunately too rare. Maïa loved her job, learned a lot and had great colleagues, but it was not always easy. She adopted her children in Kathmandu. For the first adoption, her husband had to go get their daughter because Maïa was on a trial period at work. At the time, there was no maternity leave for adoptions, which caused her more than one inconvenience when it came to picking up her son for the second adoption. "The adoption process was blocked with Nepal, and I had to stay there longer than expected. I found myself on the phone with the human resources director (a woman) who told me: 'You have to come back. We will not be able to keep your job any longer.' This blackmail made me sick, literally. I have always wanted to work, I flourish as a mother and a wife, but also in my work. I hung up and called my boss, one of the group's vice-presidents. I explained the situation, she called the company number two. She called me back the next day and told me to take the time, stay in Kathmandu and come back with my son. On my return I see the HRD because I was raised and promoted after being away for months; she said to me: 'Anyway, we know how you got there,' insinuating that I had slept my way up the ladder." There are times when solidarity among women could benefit from some progress.

Being a mother and an entrepreneur

> *Your time is limited, so don't waste it living someone else's life.*
>
> —Steve Jobs

We had trouble recruiting women's startups for The Refiners, especially because the program involved going to the United States for three months, which tends to leave women with young children on the sidelines. I'm glad in the September to December 2018 cohort, we managed to get five female co-founders out of 11 companies we onboarded. Fathers, on the other hand, seem not to have the same scruples about leaving their children in France with their partner. We had a case where the whole family moved to follow the parent entrepreneurs. In another case, the new mother wanted to come with her two-month-old baby, but the husband did not want to stay away from the child for three months, and the woman suddenly passed the CEO hat to her partner.

We interviewed Marion Carrette in mid-December 2017. At the time, she wanted to move to Marseille on a full-time basis, which meant she would have to give up the chairmanship of OuiCar, to be nothing more than a stockholder and member of the Supervisory Board. For nearly four years, she had split her time between family and work: her home was in Marseille and she spent Monday to Thursday in Paris. The company considered moving its headquarters to Marseille, but this represented too great a disruption for her teams. Marion has two sons (aged 7 and 11 in 2017) and has always put her family first. As a child, she grew up in Lille, but her father worked in Paris. This family set-up had not particularly disturbed her, and she could easily imagine going back and forth between Paris and Marseille. "When I had children, I panicked," says Marion. "I did my best work at night, and I had never worked on weekends. I liked to work late and bring nothing home. What was I going to do? There was a short adaptation phase. But that's why the three and a half years going to Paris suited me so well. I like to make the most of things, including when that means going through an intense period to then be able to enjoy things to the fullest. Today, I have a perfect balance, with a job that I love, teams I choose, and we live on the seaside. This sense of fulfillment shows. I am not very stressed by nature, and I manage to separate my personal and professional worlds. For a very long time, I felt bad because I did not think about work on weekends, then I realized that this was an incredible strength—we should not burn ourselves out." As a result, Marion is an example of reassuring leadership. Her teams feel that they can rely on this quiet strength. She is serious, but grounded. Her calm infuses the company's overall spirit.

It's not always easy to reconcile maternity and entrepreneurship, but I strongly believe that it is useless to force ourselves to adopt a rhythm or an attitude that is not natural to us. If you need to dedicate a lot of time to your work and that's what makes you happy, your children will accept it. Children absorb everything—what is going well and what is not. For my part, I think I would have been a bad mother if I had not worked. The important thing is to own your choices.

"When women entrepreneurs tell me that they do not have time to have children, I tell them that we never have time to have children," said Corinne Vigreux in our interview on April 18, 2018. She is the founder of TomTom, the Dutch company that has made a name for itself by manufacturing mobile GPS products. Corinne found the time for children, making certain sacrifices, but without any regrets. When her children were born, TomTom was growing, and since she was in charge of the whole business, she did not really have the time to take maternity leave. Being her own boss allowed her some flexibility. "The whole time they were little, I never saw friends. It was so exciting to start a business and have children that there was no place for anything else. But that was never a frustration, because I felt fulfilled. I loved what I was doing." In the early days, she held many work meetings at home. Her children grew up immersed in the entrepreneurial adventure, taking it in like mother's milk. The children saw that running a business is not a long calm river, but they also saw the passion. Her youngest son is founding a business in turn —she passed on the passion.

On November 22, 2017, I interviewed Rachel Delacour, a mother and entrepreneur with a beautiful, inspiring journey that says a lot about possibilities. While she was raising a family, she set up her business with her husband in the south of France and sold it to Zendesk, the global leader in customer support, in October 2015 for $45 million. Rachel has two young children. After the acquisition she worked for Zendesk until October 2018, but decided not to move to San Francisco and to stay in Montpellier. She led a brisk life. Constraints pushed her to be creative and organized. Based in Montpellier, she set up a routine of trips to Silicon Valley that were entirely dedicated to work. She's been to San Francisco forty times and barely knows the city. For her, reconciling a professional life guided by a great sense of urgency and family life requires logistics and planning. "As a mom, you need military-like discipline—you shouldn't ask too many questions. I explained it to the children very early on. I think even babies can understand. I want to set an example —we have to work, and work often requires traveling. I am lucky to have a husband who helps me a lot. As CTO, he has a very local role. It was natural for me to be the representative. The fact that he stays in Montpellier more helps a lot. Now that we work less together, he helps me in the development of my personal career. You have to be two to take care of children."

Not everyone has a spouse who provides so much support when making the choice of being both an entrepreneur and a mother. "As women, we have to prove ourselves more, but above all there are 2,000 years of habit making women the ones who still manage everyday life," says Fanny Bouton during our interview on January 22, 2018. She followed her husband to Hong Kong and the three years she spent there accelerated her career, but proved to be the beginning of the end of her relationship. "My husband asked me to stop working many times. It is still difficult for some men to see their women shine, especially in a masculine environment. There were a lot of problems with jealousy. I gave everything I could to my relationship, my children, the housework and more. I was home every day from 4 p.m. to 8 p.m. and spent all day Wednesday with the kids. When they were in bed I went back to work."

This is what Caroline Ramade calls "the worst possible day for women"—work full on for a day, leave in the middle of the afternoon and return to work again from 9 p.m. until 2 a.m. When Caroline's two children were four and seven, her companion was doing his part taking care of the family, to such an extent that she felt an imbalance coming and decided to set limits so she could accompany her children every morning to school. This involved promoting other collaborators. "My goal was to have people other than me represent the association. I do not want to be a muse, that's not my point. My vision is to find people better than me on this or that subject and to learn to delegate."

Indeed, rebalancing could be necessary. Children adapt if their parents are happy, and parents can trust their intuition to feel when things are not going well—you just have to listen.

Helen Bouygues is Franco-American and living in France. An entrepreneur who sold her business, she has worked for a long time for firms like McKinsey as an expert in business turnaround. There are fewer than ten people in France who do her job and, globally, extremely few women are associates in firms of this size. Women on the board say there is a lot of work, that crisis management and company turnarounds require one to be there. The assignments are intense and occur in the customer's business. This excludes many women who want to raise a family, not to mention that young people entering the sector find few examples of inspiring women, because the environment is very masculine. Helen has an extremely combative temperament, she enjoys winning clients, and can pitch all day long. She needs a lot of intellectual stimulation, which she gets from her work, but she has been lured too far into hyperactivity. She admits how important it is to listen when you start feeling that it's time to let things go and that the current balance is no longer working. At the same time, she says you need to own your choices in a society which tries to make the mothers feel guilty.

"From a traditional point of view," she says, "I chose the worst time to start my company—my daughter was three months old. The trigger was partly financial, partly the desire to have my independence. I was the only woman among fifty associates in Europe. I did not feel treated well during my pregnancy. I had planned to return a month after the birth. A single, childless male partner told me, 'My grandfather was a pediatrician, I know you're not coming back full time, and certainly not in a month.' I stopped a week before giving birth, and customers were calling me to tell me that my colleague was inviting them to lunch in August. He wanted to poach them. I decided that I did not want to work in an environment like that.

"When my daughter was 7 years old, I decided not to feel guilty and to give her as much time as I could. In 2016, I traveled outside of France a total of 216 days. My husband said, 'I would like not to have to talk to your assistant to know when we can have dinner together at home.' I was caught up on a treadmill that I alone could slow down. I deliberately decided to spend more time with my daughter and do things I had never done before. My job is purely left brain, I started to explore my right brain. I hired a coach, I was very involved in volunteering, mentoring startups. I turned to young people, including women working at McKinsey, even after leaving the firm. Right now, I am writing a book on critical thinking [New Critical Thinking: The Rise of Technology and Why Everyone Needs to Question Everything]. Yet, what I like to do is turn around failing companies. But I will not sacrifice my family and friends on the altar of my career. I deeply believe that we know deep down when the opportunity deserves making sacrifices." Today, Helen's daughter is very proud that her mother is also the parent representative for her class.

The value of work has structured Delphine Bellini's whole life. She is now general manager of the fashion house Schiaparelli. In our interview on March 14, 2018, she explained that she learned the value of work from her father, an engineer and entrepreneur. "My father always showed us that what forges success is work—a passion for the job, the work, the tenacity," she says. As a result, it is important for her to share the place that work occupies in her life with her young son. "Since he was little, I have talked a lot with my son. I have always explained honestly why I have to leave or come back late, that I have responsibilities and duties towards my company, my boss, my coworkers, that it is important to deliver on your commitments and to put heart and effort into doing what needs to be done."

Entrepreneurship blurs boundaries between professional and personal life. Hélène Duval, the founder of the yoga clothing brand YUJ, comes from a family of retailers. She was not surprised to discover that when you are an entrepreneur, you necessarily take your whole family with you. As a branded entrepreneur, she fully embodies her project, even more than her husband does his business—he is a service contractor. Being her own boss, Hélène enjoys a certain freedom in the management of her time, which facilitates her life as mother of three young children aged three, seven and nine. She explained in our interview on December 18, 2017, that she was also able to choose offices very close to her children's school, so she wouldn't lose an hour in the commute. "The most restrictive thing is homework. A coach helps kids do their homework on Monday. Every Sunday afternoon, we do homework together for three or four hours. We must be extremely well organized."

I greatly admire the tenacity of Sibylle de Villeneuve. Mother of two older boys, she has raised her children alone since the second was five months old, without any external financial support. Her big gamble was to leave her day job. How would she raise two children without a penny to her name and working day and night? Her conclusion was that when you do not have a choice, you figure things out, with more or less resilience. "When you have the energy, you do it. I did not ask myself a lot of questions. I was taught not to complain. At home, saying 'I'm tired' was the worst thing you could say. It's a matter of education. In my family, five out of five children are like that. I always laugh a little when I see friends exhausted while they have nannies. I have always been on time at school. I did have a mother I could count on when my children were sick, which happened often, because they went to the nursery and then to public school. I lived my life as an entrepreneur without ever slacking in my role as a mother—it never got put on the back burner. My sons are the only people for whom I can afford to go on a date. The days are longer, of course." Like many women, without the computer revolution, it would have been much harder for her to achieve what she did—her computer allowed her to work from home and to work in the mornings and evenings. During the whole period I was managing LeWeb from San Francisco, we worked together remotely. For Sibyl, pregnancies have never dampened productivity in women. On the contrary, children contribute to maintaining a personal balance. "Children are incredible safeguards, and drivers. When you have children, you are more careful about what you do. If I sink, I bring two others underwater with me. It's like a plant with stakes as support, and I don't know who is the plant and who is the stake."

Prioritizing organization

For every minute spent in organizing, an hour is earned.

—Benjamin Franklin

Having time to yourself is a very personal issue. For me, the time I devote to my family is personal time, while time spent alone depresses me more than it soothes me. My personal flourishing comes for the most part through family, which takes priority over everything else. That's why I'm an entrepreneur—it allows a certain amount of freedom. I have always found psychological comfort knowing that if I have to do something, I can. I am the one who decides. In 2003-2004, I rented offices next to my apartment. When my eldest son was in sixth grade, after school he would come to the office rather than return to an empty apartment. Being able to work five minutes from home is a real luxury, and not only from a psychological point of view. Your career comes and goes. It is an important dimension in life, but you build it as you go along. You can have real influence over how it is designed. However, there is no turning back in family life. I believe that it's the little details of everyday life that build a family. I do not believe in spending only a few hours a week of quality time with your children—that is something we do when we can't do otherwise.

Mathilde Thomas is one of my old friends from SKEMA. In 1994, she created the cosmetics brand Caudalie with her husband, Bertrand. Not only did they give birth to a very beautiful brand of cosmetics, they also had three children, who, at the time I interviewed her on March 27, 2018, were 10, 14 and 16 years old. They needed flawless organization to lead their entrepreneurial adventure at the same time as their family life. "I know my schedule a year in advance, day by day, hour by hour, and I've always had a great nanny—that's the secret. We limit social events, have breakfast and dinner with our children, and we spend a lot of time on vacation and weekends raising them. We travel a lot, so it's not uncommon for us to be away one week a month. We are fortunate here to have our family nearby to look after them."

For Clementine Piazza, founder of InMemori, life is a whole, and the course of action that we give ourselves will apply to both the professional side and the personal side. From her perspective, it's not so much about managing time as ensuring quality of time—are we really available, fully present with the person in front of us? When you decide not to be subject to time but to own it, false priorities fade away. It is easy to remove 50 percent of what is clogging up our schedule by eliminating what is not essential to your life project or is an opportunity to boost someone else. This applies to what happens in companies that count time. "A manager who thinks that a good employee is the one who gives seven fifths of his time is not doing the right analysis. What is better, five fifths of someone no good or four fifths of someone very good? Women always want to have a good conscience. In large companies, when they start to have children, they decide they won't have time to do the job right. As a result, managers aged 35 are men. Obviously, it is not two more hours a day that will change things."

When we started our second business, I had two children. I would leave the office no later than 6 p.m. My ex-husband thought it would never work. But it went very well.

Recently, in France there has been a lot of talk about mental load. Many women are at work, but keep their cell phones in their pockets, waiting for a text message from their child who is taking the bus home alone. The personal and professional worlds are constantly intermingling. According to the psychiatrist Aurélia Schneider, men and women would be equally impacted by the mental load, were it not for women's chronobiological rhythm, clocked by hormones secreted every 60 to 90 minutes, which predispose women to overload. We spend our lives reading the environment by calculating everything and planning constantly.

For me, organization is a keystone that holds together the whole of my personal and professional life. It's in my character, but I also think it's a choice. The more organized we are, the less we feel caught unprepared when imponderables arrive. I never procrastinate, I always try to complete what I have to do as soon as possible. Even though I receive hundreds of emails a week, I answer everything, and I have never had a personal assistant—I do it all myself. I can only do it because I have a clear routine ordered by my priorities.

Amira Yahyaoui has a mode of operation quite similar to mine. She sets a lot of overall objectives, but no daily goals. Her list of things to do must fit on one page, and she prunes what runs over. Every morning she takes out her pen and writes down her to-do list on a piece of paper and rewrites it until it fits into one page. Her e-mail box only holds the messages that have just arrived. She keeps things a clean as possible. "When I wake up, I make my bed. I wear makeup every day. I like organization, be it in people, tasks, or a startup."

I get up at 6 a.m. I like to have time in the morning to get the machine running. In general, I take 45-minute lunch breaks to meet people. I try to see a lot of people. I attend many conferences. I travel often and regularly go to Paris. When I do something, I devote myself entirely to it. I'm multitasking, but sequentially.

Here is a tiny anecdote. We organized the pitch night event for The Refiners. Instead of asking for help from my partners or me, the colleague organizing it, although full of goodwill, mistakenly thought it would be possible to print 400 badges at the last minute. Of course, there are a lot of last-minute things you do not anticipate when you organize an event. So, everything that can be done upstream must be done ahead of time. We found ourselves putting out several small fires before they turned into disasters. In other words, if you have a deadline, if you know there is a need, do not wait until the last minute. In events, there are numerous reasons to stress. On the day of the event, the security committee passes at 7 a.m. to give you permission to host your participants. You have to be able to handle all manner of emergency, such as being told that you cannot open because there is some security issue. There are so many parameters to take into account. A successful event results from micro-details that cannot be foreseen. As is often said, the devil is in the details. The content and the editorial line are essential too, of course. I often say that in entrepreneurship, the idea counts less than execution. A good checklist can drastically improve the results.

Rania Belkahia co-founded Afrimarket, often touted as the African Amazon. She also considers organization to be an essential parameter: "I have plenty of entrepreneurial friends who are overwhelmed because they do not get themselves organized. At first, I gave everything to Afrimarket. For three years, my co-founder and I did not take any vacation. In the beginning, you have to give everything. We put all our energy towards advancing, convincing the first partners and the first employees. We were physically exhausted, like zombies. Then came the second phase, when we could take two weeks of vacation a year. The business was starting to grow, we are starting to have cohorts, to make sales, to set up internal procedures. Today, we have a staff of 170 people. We had to reinvent ourselves at each stage, to evolve personally at the same pace, even faster than our company. We needed to organize our company as well as our lives and our minds to achieve our goal. This requires a lot of anticipation, including when it comes to personal organization." Rania was 28 years old at the time of the interview on March 13, 2018. She has a lot of physical energy she needs to channel. She does exercise every day. She says her first sport is her business, but she started running after her first year of entrepreneurship. Today, she runs to work, getting in ten kilometers every morning, from the sixth to the eighteenth arrondissement of Paris. Here running time is the only moment she does not answer the phone.

Everyone needs to find her own outlet and what will feed the balance. As far as I'm concerned, my energy secret is sleep. These days, people tend to neglect sleep, but I make sure to get at least seven hours a night. In the United States, it's easy to go to bed early —it's cultural, the dinners start at 7 p.m., whereas French people usually dine around 8 p.m. To sleep, you need to tire yourself physically. I walk a lot. And I never drink alcohol.

Balance

> *Yesterday is but a dream, tomorrow a vision. But today well lived makes every yesterday a dream of happiness, and every tomorrow a vision of hope. Look well, therefore, to this day.*
>
> —Sanskrit proverb, quoted by Clementine Piazza

On the Japanese island of Okinawa, known for the longevity of its inhabitants, there is no word for retirement. On the other hand, its inhabitants have an *ikigai*, a "reason for being." This concept, which is the subject of many very detailed books, completely resonates with my way of operating. My interpretation is that we decide to follow the path that we take by putting ourselves at the center of the equation, not in an egocentric and selfish way, but rather in a spirit of balance between all facets of life. Once you have set a course, it is a kind of compass that can realign you. It evolves quite a bit. In this way, it is easier to find the means to succeed based on our own criteria.

To find your *ikigai*, start by asking yourself the following questions: What do you like? What are you good at? What can you bring to the world? For what can you be paid? At the crossroads of the answers to these four questions lies the germ of your *ikigai*. Ask yourself what motivates you to do things, identify the contexts in which you shine, take the time to make your choices. And accept that it can change. "It's as important to be on the right road as not to get lost on the wrong one for years," Clémentine Piazza told us. "It was a woman who told me that when I was about to go into consulting, 'You can learn from consulting, but so what? If that's not what you want in 15 years, you're wasting your time, and happiness does not wait.' When I started my business, I felt aligned, stronger."

Based on what he learned from Andy Grove at Intel, engineer and venture capitalist John Doerr authored the book *Measure What Matters* about the OKR *(Objectives and Keys Results)* system. This method, proven in companies such as Google or LinkedIn, is used extensively and is ultimately easily applicable on a personal basis. It aims to define objectives with key, and above all, realistic and measurable results. It is not a question of aiming for the moon, but of reaching a sum of concretely attainable objectives. OKRs are usually defined at the macro level of the company and in teams with the intention of aligning and focusing effort. We put the method in place for startups that are in the Refiners program. Every week, we have partner reviews and ask them to set tangible goals and achieve them. For them, it's important because it creates milestones, which helps them stay on course and see progress even when the latter is not so visible. This method is also easy to transpose into everyday life on a personal level. For my part, I apply it more or less intuitively without really realizing it, because it corresponds perfectly to my mode of operation.

My personal motto is that happiness is a decision you make. For Myriam Maestroni, it is cultivated; it is a path full of hardships, where everyone has the choice to fall down or to bounce back. Destiny is the science of choices and consequences.

Myriam has lived a lot in a world of men. At the age of 24, she became the general manager of a company that distributed petroleum products and, after six years, she moved on to Agip to work in refining, before recreating Primagaz from scratch. In 2003, after living in Spain and the Netherlands, she returned to France where she was appointed sales director of Primagaz. Upon arrival, the business was losing more customers than it was taking on. She realized that what seems simple never is. In a world of energy centered on logistics, security of supply, the price of oil and geopolitical sensitivity, the customer asked only one question: how much does it cost per month? Myriam is a graduate in natural medicine as well as in business management. She understood that the future was in energy efficiency. In 2004, she set the cat among the pigeons announcing that she will help customers consume less.

"When you are the only woman on the executive committee of a company whose business model for the past 100 years has been based on increasing consumption, and that you come up with something that assertive, you hear everything, including 'And she's blonde on top of that,'" said Myriam. "Despite that, there were people who followed me. In the end, I learned a lot. People always say that one-third of people change, one-third of people need a push, and one-third of people do not budge. I found the percentage of people I needed for the business to change." In 2004, she launched energy consulting. In 2006, laws changed and energy companies had to help their customers consume less. Myriam was relieved, because you cannot be right all alone for too long. But with that, her strategy of differentiation, based on accompanying the customer to consume less but be happier for a longer time, went up in smoke. She decided to devote the passion she had put into energy consulting into a site that was born in 2008, becoming www.economiedenergie.fr, an intrapreneurial project within Primagaz. She nonetheless remained general manager of a company with more than 1,000 employees, with problems of industrial safety and declining sales.

In 2011, the group began to diversify. A crisis of succession at the head of the company and a series of circumstances led her to realize that she would never rise higher. Primagaz was one of the largest companies in the group, and she saw clearly that it is impossible to appoint a French woman to the board of directors of a Dutch company with 99 percent men. Myriam was still young (43 years old), and she decided to leave. Ten people told her they wanted to continue the work started on energy consulting. Myriam managed to negotiate a spinoff of www.economiedenergie.fr, which at the time was only a site and has become an international consultancy specialized in improving energy efficiency. "It was bits of ideas backed by strong convictions. The company was born from a real gamble that shattered the sectoral practices that I found no longer worked. Today, it is a comprehensive market that touches one out of every two homes in France."

In 2018, Économie d'énergie was working with major French retailers as well as banks. The company brought together 180 people, with absolute parity, all trades combined. For 15 years, Myriam had been almost the only woman (with two others who did not stay so long) in the top 100 of a large corporation. "Today, with hindsight, I wonder how I was able to survive for 15 years. I should get a medal! It is even scandalous that we continue to tolerate companies operating like that." In her company, Myriam has set up a cross-entity project far removed from the silos she had known. She has a holistic approach to the business in her ecosystem. In 2004, when she launched the consultancy, Économie d'énergie published its first sustainable development report without being obliged to do so. Myriam put multiple factors into the equation that she found important to reconcile. "I was fascinated by oil, this resource the earth offers us. I would not have worked if I could not align my mission with my work. You have to have a life that matches your ideas, otherwise you have to change your life or your ideas. I believe in alignment, and being kind, happy, and intelligent. Women have a holistic vision, they know how to think by putting a lot of things in the equation. Digital can reflect holistic thinking. It brings ubiquity and speed, the outcome of an iterative thought. This is essential in energy efficiency, where there are five levers with ten criteria conditioning each one."

Human life has only existed for 200,000 years, and it is fragile. When Myriam began her reflection in 2003, she had a great awareness of this fragility, even though she had no idea that climate change issues would accelerate so much. The threat to humanity today must be an invitation to live as much as possible in line with your values. "If one of us makes a difference with one percent of humanity, the world is saved. There are things that cannot be bought

—the values we give ourselves. Convictions carry us beyond money. I have always lived with the idea that a life is finite. We have one certainty: one day, we die. When we look back on our life, we can have remorse, but not regrets. At the time of the assessment, the choices we made make a destiny. This helps to bring relativity to difficulties that seem insurmountable. My grandmother, who just turned 103, said, 'Living is a full-time job and you learn everything except how to live.' Man or woman, let's make sure we lead our lives fully in its many dimensions. There are seven billion of us and we all have unique destinies. Let's focus on the gift of a life rather than jealousy over the neighbor's destiny. In the end, there is a fabulous remedy to all fear, and that is courage. What comes from courage makes our humanity. All the rest, which dominates, is infra-human."

Chapter 3

Choosing a Direction and Staying on Course

From passion to vision

The future belongs to those who believe in the beauty of their dreams.

—Eleanor Roosevelt

My Little Paris grew from Fany Pechiodat's passion for Paris. She didn't say, "I'm going to start a business." Rather, she spontaneously followed her passion all the way. That is why after the French digital media group aufeminin bought out her startup, she stayed on to lead the venture until the private national French TV channel TF1 took over in 2017. Throughout all nine years of her entrepreneurial adventure, there was not a single day that she did not want to get up to go to work. Now, she has moved on to create her new startup Seasonly.

I interviewed Fany in October 2017. She told me how much she loved wandering the streets of Paris looking for the city's best-held secret spots. In 2008, while she was working at Jean-Paul Gaultier in marketing, she and her sister decided to send a first newsletter to a group of 50 friends to share the good addresses they had discovered. In only six months, through word of mouth, she had 10,000 subscribers. That is when she decided to launch a startup, and she resigned from her salaried job a year later. "I said to myself, if you don't do this, you'll miss out on your life. Don't miss out on your life out of laziness or fear, even when that means turning left when you had planned to turn right. You need to have a life that matches who you are as closely as possible, one that stems from pleasure." Fany's vision was more of an ideal than an entrepreneurial big picture. She wanted people to fall in love with Paris. She was just as passionate about bringing emotion to the digital world, which she did by getting illustrator Kanako Kuno onboard to illustrate the newsletter. Later, when she decided to create My Little Box, a beauty and lifestyle box, she wanted to do something entirely unlike Amazon. Instead of receiving an invoice in a soulless cardboard box, customers received a package wrapped in ribbon. She ended up with 150,000 subscribers. Her ideal was the primary driver, not the figures (be it the number of subscribers or the sales figures), even though growth very quickly became a game for her.

One of the motivators for leaving her job and launching the business was the impact she had on people's lives by talking about them. "I found an extremely talented Chinese massage therapist. She received 2,000 calls the day we mentioned her in a newsletter. She founded her own business and hired four people. When we talked about some subway musicians, one of them was contacted by a producer to record an album. These 'little stories' are at the very heart of My Little Paris—recommendations, on a micro-local level, shared with authenticity." At the beginning, people told Fany that her business couldn't scale as long as it was linked to her personality, her sister's writing style and Kanako's graphic style. It nevertheless managed to grow without ever doing any advertising, because she never left the path of her vision.

"At the time, newsletters were a disaster. I based mine on the kind of newsletter I wanted to receive. I wanted it to be readable in one minute. I told our writers to write as if they were sharing with their best friend. Their job was to write to 4 million women, but one by one." My Little Paris newsletters often have a poetic dimension, such as the most beautiful trees in Paris, or the best bench in Paris for making a decision. In 2017, My Little Paris had ten or so finders, assisted by a person responsible for filtering the information and putting it on the right publication track (newsletter, Instagram, etc.). "It's hard to find people who are a little obsessional. There are not that many people who will bundle up and go out in the middle of the winter cold to uncover something new. I will never tell you about a place you already know. I was always looking for new spots, like some people look for mushrooms in the woods. Sundays, I would leave the house at eight in the morning and get home at midnight. When it became a full-time job, I didn't know what to do on Sundays to recharge my batteries."

When the question of monetization arose, Fany refused to deface her newsletter with ad banners. She preferred to gamble on creativity, by reinventing ads to create value for her community. To do so, she needed to convince the luxury brands to play along, which managed to do.

Passion combined with hard work can go very far, but only if you believe in the pertinence of your vision enough to give your life to it. My Little Paris did a survey one day asking its readers if they had some project on the back burner that they didn't dare to undertake because they lacked self-confidence—be it a business, a book or an Etsy shop. Ninety-two percent of the women responded yes.

"The hardest moment is the one when you ask yourself if you're really going to take the step and found your business," Fany says. "Once you've done so, you find the energy to move mountains. The smallest thing can help to take that step, be it a sentence heard at a conference, or a discussion with a friend. Often, we are looking for a sign that it is time."

Passion is also what led Barbara Belvisi to found the Hardware Club in 2015. It's a mix between an investment fund and a startup club specialized in hardware (producing electronic objects, robots, connected objects, etc.). As a kid, Barbara spent her time fixing things up with her father, who was a musician, and studying science with her mother, who was a jurist. She played the chemist and the electrician, while composing on the piano. Surrounded by this creative atmosphere as a child, she already had the idea that she would create something. She attended EMLyon Business School, where she discovered finance and decided to pursue that as a career, first specializing in fusions and acquisitions and then in capital risk. Afterwards, she wanted to create her own fund. In 2012, seeing the first wave of hardware startups spreading throughout the ecosystem, she determined that the time was right. For a full year, she picked up her pilgrim's staff and began to prospect and consult startups with the ultimate goal of creating a fund. Her vision was to create a community at the heart of it all, so she set her priority to build a community of values and ideas from which to raise funding. "Everything you give to an ecosystem comes back around. I am fascinated by communities, ecosystems and the power of bringing people together around causes. These are ideas that nourish me. I'm animated by the model and the approach, the idea of gathering people together to create something powerful." At the time of our interview at the end of 2017, the Hardware Club was accompanying 370 startups throughout the world, with a selection rate of five to six percent, bringing together a community of more than 200 large business partners to lower the risk of its investments.

Passion is no less important when building a career outside of entrepreneurship. For Isabelle Bordry, who was managing director at Yahoo! France, you should give yourself a maximum of possibilities to turn your passion into your career. It is hard to be successful in something that doesn't fit you. Our pleasure zone is also often our zone of excellence. Isabelle chose to follow what interested her rather than fitting into a mold. When she finished her degree at the Paris-Dauphine University, one of France's top school, all her classmates when on to auditing. It was the big trend at the time. But Isabelle took another tangent. It was the media that attracted her. She joined Hachette Filipacchi, where she learned the workings of the press. In 1995-1996, Hachette started being interested in multimedia and decided to offer its main titles on the Internet. The business brought together teams of passionate young people to create and deploy its brands on the Internet. Isabelle started selling ad banners, even though she had switched to multimedia to avoid selling ads. She continued to work on subjects that interested her and followed opportunities, until one day she got a call from Yahoo!—they were starting to develop on the European market. In 1997, she became their sixth employee in Paris. Her colleagues at Hachette thought she was crazy going to join a small business, but she knew that if she wanted to follow the Internet idea all the way, it was important to be part of a business that did only that. She believed strongly in this new media. In 1997, she put together a sales team and joined the general management in the early 2000s. When she left Yahoo! at the end of 2005, she was the youngest member of the European management team, but the person who had been in the company the longest. Google had already prevailed.

From October 2013 to July 2015, Isabelle became vice-president of the grassroots political party Nous Citoyens, heading up the list for the Ile-de-France region in the 2014 European elections. Politics were in her family culture. At the time of the 2014 European elections, she wanted to run against the far-right Front National movement, aligning with her view of the economy. "I thought that traditional political parties were largely responsible for the rise of extremist parties because they were so timid when it came to Europe. Also, at the time, there was a kind of fatality regarding political action and their capacity to change and make people's lives better. A lot of people were explaining that politics didn't change anything. And when I went into areas outside of the cities, I realized that unemployment was high, particularly among young people, and it was aggravating the lack of social integration. To unlock employment, we needed to reform the labor code and the education system. During the political meetings I attended in 2014, I realized how young women in these areas were outside the doors of the economy. Many of them asked for help, gave me their resumés, because unlike other politicians I debated with, I represented the economy. Politicians and entrepreneurs share a passion to change things. You display this desire in full view of all when you want to be in the government or to be an elected official or to head a company. Countless entrepreneurs have transformed the world and the way it works. Unlike what some may think, money, although important, is not a key motivator in an entrepreneurial approach. Money often comes only after numerous failures and hard times. A sincere entrepreneur is not necessarily someone who wants to earn money. In politics, money cannot be a lever—the only driver possible is to support public life. And this is where entrepreneurs and politicians come together. This mechanism really fascinated me. Money aside, the real difference between politics and entrepreneurship is getting your face on a poster and becoming a public figure."

There is a way of being an entrepreneur that comes from building projects with other men and women, rolling up your sleeves and sharing your vision. Being an employee can also be a huge human and entrepreneurial adventure. As an employee and a consultant, on several occasions Delphine Bellini experienced the same thing entrepreneurs do when building and growing their businesses. She led projects, raised funding, structured teams, implemented tools and processes, and reported to single or multiple shareholders. All of these experiences held great lessons about people, operations, and finance, and forged her spirit. The way she took over the Schiaparelli fashion house is an expression of a very strong intrepreneurial vision. "What interests me is creating value with a team, creativity in its purest form, and know-how. Schiaparelli had extremely fertile ground arising from the history and heritage of this illustrious fashion house founded in 1927 by Elsa Schiaparelli, a creative genius, a visionary, and a fabulous female entrepreneur. To be inspired and to inspire others, to share a vision and strong convictions, to create a whole ecosystem to serve a project and aim for excellence with the sole goal of enchanting people—that is how you build, develop and sustain projects. All the projects I have had the opportunity to participate in are filled with these."

What woman will you be in five years?

Set objectives, but do not calculate. Remain curious and open to opportunities—you do not know where life will lead you.
—Frédérique Dame, Partner Google Venture

Personally, I work with objectives. What do I want to accomplish in my overall life, in one month, in the week, today? I don't write them down, but I keep them in my mind, and they allow me to make decisions.

Here is a silly example. At the beginning of August 2017, I had to interrupt my vacation in France and return to San Francisco because I was summoned for my interview to get American citizenship. I had two possibilities. I could go back to the United States and then return to France or I could just say to myself, "I'm in San Francisco in August, how can I make the most of it?" Everyone knows the comment attributed to Mark Twain about being in San Francisco during summertime: "The coldest winter I ever spent was a summer in San Francisco." It would leave me a whole month to exercise and take some time for myself. I tested some gyms, and I did yoga every day. I focused on myself for myself. I never usually have time to exercise every day. I was able to make of the most of that month because I had one goal, which was to be in the best possible shape to go back to work.

As it turns out, over the past five years, I have had to completely change my vision. I am at a turning point. My youngest son, who is seventeen, is in the process of leaving home. During the last five years, I focused on the necessity of completely rebuilding my career by doing things differently. When I divorced, the youngest of my three teenagers was twelve years old, so I couldn't get it wrong. I channeled all my energy into reframing my life around these circumstances. I had to weigh risks and opportunities that presented themselves at the present time without asking metaphysical questions.

It is interesting to give yourself a direction. "What choices should I make now?" Continuing to learn is key. I learned a lot by creating The Refiners. I only knew about investment from the point of view of a business angel, and I discovered the fundamental difference between investing with other people's money and with your own.

Delphine Bellini never made a career plan. Chance encounters and opportunities guided her steps. But, mostly, it was work, passion and achievements that formed her career path. She nevertheless recommends to students she accompanies to "reverse engineer their resume" by asking the following question: "What do you want to be at the end of your career? What would you like to accomplish or become? To get there, what do you need to do, what steps to you need to climb, and what do you need to learn? "It is not talent that leads to success, but work," says Delphine. "Nor is it a question of intelligence, but rather of personal commitment and conviction. That is what allows you to always move forward."

Alice Guilhon, dean of SKEMA Business School, built her career by advancing from one challenge to another. Born into an academic family, she was made for working in education. As a child, she wanted to become a teacher, but she suffered serious cardiac problems that made it difficult to make long-term projections. As a result, she did a many, many things while she was young in order to make the most of the time she had—from music at the conservatory to competition tennis. When Alice was ten, her trainer saw her potential, and Alice said to herself, "I'm going to show them what I can do." Working with a top coach, she developed her tenacity and ranked very well. At the age of sixteen, she competed in the French Open, became completely burned out and ended up in a coma. She stopped playing tennis. From there, she went back to a more traditional path of studies. When she studied economics at the university, she was more or less looking for meaning. She set the challenge of getting her doctorate as young as possible, and she presented her dissertation at the age of twenty-five. The next goal was to become a university professor, which she did, and then she quickly got bored. She had a child, did research, and got bored again. Thanks to a friend, she got a job at the Ministry of the Interior and specialized in economic intelligence. Then she wanted to return to live in her home town of Nice. A friend from HEC Business School gave her the idea of working at one of France's elite schools. In 2000, she visited what was then the CERAM Business School (it later became SKEMA following a merger with another school) and said, "I'm going to turn this into something out of the ordinary." She didn't know where to begin, but she knew what her next challenge would be. "I wanted to make it a leading research school. In 2000-2005, France's elite *grandes écoles* were becoming real rivals to the universities. For me, the general direction never was the final outcome. When people got in the way, I said to myself, 'They have to go because they are not the right people.' I fought fiercely to get European Quality Improvement System accreditation. I went to see the Chamber of Commerce and Industry telling them that I had a grand project that would change the world of higher education. There were only men, but they let me do my thing. I had long dreamed about shaking up the world. If you have a little ambition, you can be disruptive in a world that doesn't innovate. My project was comprehensive. When we decided on the merger, people laughed. But it worked like a dream. The challenge I set was to carry SKEMA very far, and I will not let go until it's done." And Alice still plays music.

Trusting yourself

> *The man who moves a mountain begins by carrying away small stones.*
>
> —Confucius

Hélène Duval is a fine example of how following your passion and listening to your intuition can contribute to building an impressive entrepreneurial path. She ended up in entrepreneurship via yoga. She practiced this discipline for twenty years, and when she began it was not well known by the general public. In 2008, she was thirty years old and worked for *Vogue* in the fashion brand sales development, but she began to lack challenges. When she told her husband that she planned to resign to raise their first child, he said, "Do what you want to do, but do it with passion." This sentence really resonated with Hélène, and she decided to create something related to her passion. She began by giving yoga classes to her friends. Through word of mouth, after only a few months she was working every day of the week, including weekends. That's how she became a yoga teacher, dressed all day long like a yoga teacher. As she had worked in fashion, she couldn't even consider not looking her best, and yet there were no yoga clothes in France. In New York, she got butterflies in her stomach when she saw women in leggings with yoga mats slung over their shoulder. It was 2012, and nobody believed yoga would be a market, but she had an intuition that there would be an enormous potential for clothing that was both beautiful and designed especially for yoga. "Intuition is very important for all women entrepreneurs. I talked to a lot of people about my idea and the only person who believed in it was my husband, who mentored me in entrepreneurship. I needed reassurance and resources, and he managed to provide both."

In February 2014, she registered the brand YUJ and held on tight to the conviction that this brand would only do yoga. YUJ comes from the three Sanskrit letters that mean "yoga" and represents the etymology of the word. Her main inspiration was Repetto, and had they entered the yoga market, she wouldn't have done so. So, Hélène founded the first French brand of yoga clothing. In the meantime, she had two other children, and went through a total of four births. "Founding a business is truly like giving birth—it's giving life. My business is my baby, and I'll make it grow. For a woman, it's an extra burden. We have a way of creating things that involves a lot of affect. Nobody wanted to produce for me, but when you create with the conviction that it will work, then it does. You always have to say that you are going to write a new page in your book, and that the EEG will not always be flat. Had I not practiced yoga at the time, I would have given in more than once. As often happens when you are very positive, the stars align. Like in meditation, even if it is dark at the beginning, there is always a light somewhere. Being a woman can make things easier, because seduction is a real weapon. The first trade show I attended gave me a booth."

Jumping on opportunities is key. When the director of the well-known French department store Galeries Lafayette stopped by her stand and offered her a pop-up store, she accepted. Although she had just given birth, she was at her stand from 9 a.m. to 8 p.m. and surpassed her objectives. She got moved up to the fourth floor, in front of Nike. As an entrepreneur, you have to accept to be learning all the time. It's exactly like being a mom—we don't know how to do it, nobody gives us the keys. Hélène's husband lent her part of his office. The stand was working well, but after a year, she was feeling overextended from doing it all. There comes a time you have to accept to stop. She gave up her Galeries Lafayette stand and went to see the Bon Marché department store to offer them an exclusive. They bought the brand, which brought her some comfort.

For her, a brand must have real DNA to do well. She created a charity event, the Yogis du Coeur, enabling heart surgery for poor children, and the second year YUJ organized a major event at the Grand Palais. With the company's rise in popularity, people were asking her for classes, but she didn't want to create just another yoga studio. Again in New York, she discovered an ashtanga yoga studio where people practice yoga in candlelight. She also discovered "flow," a dynamic yoga, and began to write a book on the method. "You need dreams all the time," she says. "I consider my dreams to be reality, and all my dreams come true. All of them." After a year, the book came out and, at the same time, the first flow yoga studio opened in Paris, with a new concept, infrared yoga. She took a gamble and opened it in the seventh arrondissement, despite contrary opinions, but she was convinced by the beauty of the spot. There is always a solution. She figured that if the classes didn't work out, she could always turn it into a showroom. YUJ opened a first boutique-studio with no publicity and no press coverage, but word of mouth—the best of all advertising—worked wonders. The studio took off, attracting all kinds of people, and it was profitable in six months. Hélène loves writing a new page in her life every day. The brand's idea now is to create a business addiction and a community of urban yogis. Through passion, her credo became a business quite naturally. YUJ holds retreats because Hélène personally needed moments for detox. Paris doesn't have enough teachers, so YUJ is training an army of yogis (YUJ Teacher Training).

"There is no recipe for creating a business. You can get all the advice in the world, and you'll do what you can. It has to come from deep inside of you. Like a child you desire, it will flourish," Hélène says. As you get more experience and advance your career, you will develop an instinct that will rarely be wrong. When you have an opinion, say it, and trust yourself. If you have the impression that whatever it may be is not right and should be done differently, share your point of view with those around you. And there is nothing wrong with being wrong. Trust your instincts and follow them. But be sure to always have arguments to support them.

When Reed Midem bought LeWeb, I stayed on to accompany the transition, but I didn't like not being in a leadership position. LeWeb was a startup and, in this kind of situation, you need to constantly rebound. Many of the choices we make are guided by intuition, keeping all the economic parameters in mind, of course. What is complicated in large corporations is that if you can't produce an excel sheet perfectly and if it isn't approved by a certain number of entities, you can't move forward. Yet, that takes time. Often, you can't make quick decisions. When you see what is happening, you say, "We need to jump on this train," but by the time everything is approved, the train is long gone. That is what was the most difficult for me.

Trusting your instinct is a particularly feminine strength, because we own our sixth sense. When it comes to investment decisions, Stéphanie Hospital trusts her gut feeling. "I can't say that I invest in a project if I don't want to work with the entrepreneurs," she says. "I look for sincerity, authenticity, and not appearances, which is often the case in large companies. Often people get caught up in internal politics, when there is no need for that."

For Clémentine Piazza, knowing your motivations sets the path of a lifetime. That is what guided her in the creation of InMemori in July 2017. "I began with a small beta version, intuitions, and convictions. When you lose someone close to you, it's a moment of truth, superfluous things disappear, and it is key to be deeply touched by what a family is going through in order to embody this kind of project. I felt that my intuitions were right, that it was really hard for a family who has just lost someone to gather that person's community, the people who would like to help but who don't want to interfere. When an event is a happy one, it is easy to get people together, but it is during grieving that it is more difficult to be together, even though those are the hardest moments in life. When Géraldine told me the project was ready, I needed six months to feel capable that I could do it." Because she was truly convinced of the importance of InMemori's mission, Clémentine didn't hesitate to leave her marketing director job to found the company. When you know what drives you, it is ultimately rather easy to change scenes.

The first piece of advice that Frédérique Dame would give to a woman who wanted to launch out on their own is "Nothing ventured, nothing gained." It is better to reason your way through your fears than to live with the regret of not having done something you held close to your heart. When you feel fear, rather than asking, "What am I going to do?" with the risk of getting discouraged by more or less imaginary limits, ask yourself, "Why do I want to do this?" Roadblocks come from the "how?" You will always find people who will tell you you're going to have problems. If your "why" is strong, you will make that project a non-negotiable part of your personal mission, and you will figure out how to do it well. Everything in this project will be authentically aligned with your life path. There are so many ways to go from A to B. Frédérique's "why" when she joined Uber was the quality of the team and the company's vision. When you are aligned with your values, you have no regrets, even when you fail.

Frédérique's second piece of advice is to always follow your instinct and to remain aligned with your values, even if that leads you to make unpopular decisions. You only have one life, and you are the one to live with the consequences of your choices, not others. Money and glory will never be enough to make you happy, but betraying your values and going against your gut feeling will do nothing but make you unhappy. Have strong values and a lot of self-esteem. If an opportunity does not correspond to your values, too bad. There will be another opportunity, and another, and yet another.

Advisors are not the ones who pay. Corinne Vigreux warns entrepreneurs against outside people who will willingly provide their advice. "You know your business better than anyone. Try to understand the motivations of the person consulting you and preserve your independence." You need convictions to lead a business. If five people tell you blue, while you are thinking red, it might be worthwhile to take a look at the blue, but if you have no convictions, you'll become as changeable as the weather. Listen to yourself. People told Céline Lazorthes that she shouldn't hire someone older than her and that she shouldn't join forces with a friend. She did both and has never regretted it.

Overcoming the imposter syndrome

> *Even though I had sold 70 million albums, there I was feeling like "I'm no good at this."*
> —Jennifer Lopez

My mother often teases me because I tend to think that if I succeed at something, it means that it was necessarily easy. Denigrating what we have accomplished is a very feminine failing. On March 8, 2018, Mariam Naficy, who created Minted, published an article on *Medium* entitled "#SheBrag" denouncing the problem that women never brag. We tend to consider that what we do is normal even when it is exceptional. It is time to learn to shine a light on we do rather than wait for others to discover it.

Fleur Pellerin also suffered from this female habit of self-censorship. "I had imposter syndrome. Even when I won a competitive examination, I would say, 'That was a lousy exam. It wasn't so hard.' I never came out of an exam saying, 'I succeeded.' After working for the revenue court, I was looking for some more government work. I was not at all sure of myself. I felt like people who understood the codes better than I did and were better integrated into the higher levels of public administration would have a better chance than I did to get the jobs. These are the things that condition us in our relationship to promotions and salaries. I have a hard time talking about money—not so much when it comes to investment, as that is part of my job, but I am less at ease when I need to discuss splitting capital or payment. I would have a hard time negotiating salary increases."

When Fleur worked on diversity and questions of equal representation with the NGO Club XXIe Siècle, men who were running large businesses told her that at the time of year when promotions were handed out, crowds of men would show up at the office at 7:30 a.m. wanting to share a coffee and talk, but there would never be any women. Women don't try to put themselves in the limelight or lobby for their own interests. They need to learn to do it, to stop being inhibited by this kind of behavior. These are among numerous circumstances when women ask too many questions. When Ségolène Royal ran in the Socialist Party primaries, other women Socialists said that the advantage she had over them was that she dared to run. Once again, this is due in large part to a lack of confidence in one's own capacities. "When a woman applies for a job, she asks, 'Am I going to succeed?' while a man asks, 'How am I going to succeed?' There is no shame in daring," Alice Guilhon told us.

Delphine Bellini confirmed that women tend to underestimate and doubt themselves. "I am the first to tell women who feel self-doubt that they can do it, by getting them to realize it themselves. But it is clear that we question our abilities more than men do."

Evidently, the imposter syndrome is not exclusively a feminine trait. That is what Frédérique Dame told us. "Everyone has insecurities, even those who have it all. In the end, we are all afraid of being imposters."

Be bold

> *Only those who try nothing do not succeed.*
> —Fanny Bouton, founder of 1000110

At The Refiners, when we meet startups both for investment and those involved in the program, I notice that men seem to demonstrate self-confidence by default. Women are perfectionists, wanting to cover all the bases before daring to jump in. A woman will prefer to cancel an appointment for which she does not feel prepared rather than dive in and take advantage of the opportunity. Fifty-four percent of women between the ages of 25 and 30 say they feel paralyzed by a fear of failure, compared to 46 percent of women over the age of 30. I like to say that if you don't try, then the answer is already "no." The only risk is to have a door opened, or perhaps a "yes." When we decide on a path, we have a choice to engage on it with more or less risk. For me, I am always looking for moderation. I try to measure and minimize the risks ahead of time, even if the scenario I've mapped out is often wrong and I cannot anticipate everything. I try to evaluate the level of risk I'm taking. The men I know are often more reckless. They dive right in, using a "come what may" approach.

The problem for women is that often it is not enough to be competent. We are constantly having to prove ourselves. This influences risk taking. Men will take risks more easily because they carry less guilt and judgement. When should I launch? Do I need to check my full list of ten items in order to get started? I usually aim for six out of ten. Most of the men I know will start when three or four out of ten are ready.

There is a very clear, observable difference in startups. Women generally tend to take a comprehensive approach. A female entrepreneur will assess the aspects linked to the product, the team, the organization, etc. and will feel responsible for facing all of these challenges head on. She will sometimes have trouble setting some important subjects to the side in order to handle them later. Often, she will act with a list of priorities that is a bit too long, where a man will more willingly compartmentalize tasks to concentrate on one thing at a time. In the organization of a startup, adopting a comprehensive approach is a good thing, but you need to define priorities. This is one of the areas we try to focus on with entrepreneurs who join The Refiners. Whether a project is led by a man or a woman, what is really key for it to get off on the right path is the capacity the person has to distance themselves from the product (often very reassuring for the ego) and to concentrate on the project's vision and mission. In this respect, gender-mixed teams take on their full meaning, with men and women making compromises in service of the mission and the vision.

At Orange, Stéphanie Hospital worked for years in the same team, which was led by Paul-François Fournier. While Stéphanie was on sabbatical, Paul-François took on other responsibilities in the company and when Stéphanie returned to work, many of her colleagues were targeting his position. Stéphanie presented her team and the projects they had led, but she did not apply for the position, as at the time she was thinking about leaving Orange and starting her own business. Xavier Couture, her boss's boss, said to her, "I'm going to give you the job, because you talked about your projects and your teams, not about yourself." She began managing those who had been her colleagues for four years—all of them men—and discovered all the benefits they had received, from training to raises. She wondered why she hadn't had the same. The answer was simple: she had never asked for them, because she expected them to be given spontaneously. Women have a good-student syndrome, expecting a good grade because they worked well. Still at Orange, Stéphanie was lucky enough to work with Xavier Couture, who helped her see her worth. One day he said to her, "Even at the foot of the the Mont Blanc, you could do a whole lot more." For Stéphanie, this sentence offered the moment of awareness that allowed her to drop her inhibitions. She needed to dare.

Women often put themselves too much in the other person's shoes and not enough in the center of the equation. Passively waiting for gratifications saying "They will end up seeing how well I perform" doesn't work. Heading up large corporations requires knowing how to negotiate, including for oneself. Odile Roujol says she made mistakes when she was younger. When she was marketing director, she worked a lot, getting both recognition and results, and she thought naively that payment would follow, a supposition that many women make. "I accepted an interview with the CEO of the Lauder group while I was traveling in New York, without even looking to discuss or negotiate with my general manager at the time. I said to myself that everyone would see me leave the meeting and would ask the right questions. I did get a raise and a better package, but with hindsight, I should have simply asked for it. I wanted it to be spontaneous and come from them, and that was an error in calculation."

Margaret Neale, a professor at Stanford, has demonstrated that when you give a remuneration budget to men and women managers saying, "Distribute this to whoever you want based on performance," they distribute it fairly and there is no difference between men and women. On the other hand, if they have to discuss with those who will not be happy with the raise, they will give more to men (women managers do the same!) because it is known that women do not like to negotiate and as a result, managing the relationship will be easier.

Odile's conclusion is that you need to learn to negotiate for yourself. We are excellent when it comes to negotiating for our teams, and it is a good thing to do the same for oneself, with a pragmatic approach.

Sibylle de Villeneuve never encountered any obstacles related to being a woman, and she never had the impression of being undervalued, underpaid, or scorned for being a woman. On the other hand, when she was an employee, she didn't ask for raises or training. She recognizes that even when buying something, women rarely ask for a discount. "As long as we leave space for men, they will dare to move forward unprepared," she says. "Women need to have more self-confidence. It should be forbidden to say that you are lucky when something works well. You are lucky when you find a dollar bill on the street, not when you've been successful for twenty years." Accompanying a woman like Martine Liautaud (a mentor for female entrepreneurs with The Women Initiative Foundation) in her press relations (and also accompanied herself by the WIF), Sibylle perceives a positive change. Once again, Iceland is exemplary, imposing a huge fine on companies that have unequal pay between men and women. The numbers are slow to change, but there are women in large companies who have decided to redraw the lines.

When Fanny Bouton was a child, she saw people on the television and people said to her, "Stop dreaming, that's not for you." That wasn't enough to stop her, and she went on to prove the naysayers wrong by becoming a high-tech columnist on the French television channel Game One in 2005. For her, you shouldn't be afraid of failing. "When you are a woman, you need to dare twice over. My career path is filled with moments when I said, 'Go on, the worst that can happen is that you fail.' When I see an opportunity, if I'm in a good state of mind to seize it, I go for it. I never once think I will fail. I kept pushing forward in a carefree manner. I never learned to network, but I discovered that it is important to meet people and to be interested in what they are doing, and that we could have things to do together, even if we are very different." Fanny finds that it is very important for brilliant women to be heard, that we have women role models. For more than ten years now, she has organized Fanny's Party, the Parisian geek meeting place. She says that unfortunately a lot of women refuse to share their experience or cancel their event at the last minute because they don't want to go on stage. "Women don't dare to express themselves if they don't know everything there is to know about the subject. If you know 80 percent, and your audience knows 20 percent, you give them 60 percent. Not counting that you are passionate about your subject and form counts more than the content. I accepted to teach at HEC Business School. I was crazy enough to dare to do it. Sometimes I stutter. I get skin rashes. You have to force yourself. You can always get better. I got coaching to improve my public speaking."

Maëlle Gavet is a fine example of a go-getter. I love what she has done because she gave herself the freedom to choose. Maëlle is someone who doesn't like to do things halfway. At the age of sixteen, she developed her first entrepreneurial project. She organized birthday parties in order to pay for her studies and finish off the month, and after a while the business grew so much, she had to hire people. She then created another event business in Russia, and one proposing online guides for expatriates. During her initial working years, she faced a number of limitations because she hadn't learned to make a business plan or a presentation. As she didn't want to go back to school, she decided to go against all the advice she had received to do an MBA, and instead joined the Boston Consulting Group where she worked happily for six years. Very flexible, she lived and worked in a number of places, including India, Ukraine, London, and Russia. In the latter, she worked for a small e-commerce, media and telecommunications company named Ozon. At the end of her assignment, the company asked her to join its team. At the time, Maëlle wanted to return to entrepreneurship, and she was a year and a half away from being an associate, which didn't tempt her. The opportunity seemed perfect, because she doesn't at all like the beginnings of creating a company. Maëlle likes order, procedures and scaling, not the initial reflections. At first, she was responsible for marketing and sales, and after a year, she became CEO. She stayed in the company for another five years and turned it into Russia's largest e-commerce site (today, Ozon is Russia's Amazon). She participated in creating a distribution network and an infrastructure equivalent to Fedex or UPS, which didn't exist there. Then the financial crisis hit, the ruble plummeted, and foreign investments slowed. The board gave Maëlle three objectives: scale up (mission accomplished and after five years Ozon was bringing in a little over a billion in sales), capitalize the company (mission accomplished with $250 million raised), and finally go public. That was a problem, the geopolitical context made international stock markets skittish. Maëlle handed the company over to her director of operations. She joined the Fortune 500 company Priceline, the largest online travel agency (16,000 people), which owns Booking.com, Open Table, Kayak, and a few other brands. She stepped in as number two, in charge of operations, working directly with the CEO, and then in January 2017, she left to work for Compass (an American technology and real estate company) as director of operations. Today, Maëlle lives in New York.

Maëlle is one of those women who decided and asked to be in charge, who said they were good at taking charge and that they could take the lead. She told us in our interview on February 15, 2018, "I always thought that this was how people managed their careers, and then I discovered that I was something of an exception. I was proud of that, because I was born like this. I have always had an independent personality, and it never crossed my mind to let someone else decide my career or my life. I make my choices, always with a smile, but I am always very clear about what I am capable of doing, what I am ready to do, and what I don't want to do."

Maëlle mentors several young women within Compass and outside of the company, because she is worried. She finds it extremely frustrating that there are brilliant women who never manage to reach the top of their dreams (whatever the target, which doesn't have to be CEO). She advises the women she coaches to always raise their hand, whether to ask questions (no need to make excuses when you do), when someone is looking for a volunteer for a project (even if they think they are not qualified), or when someone asks who is ready to take charge of something that nobody wants to do. "Women, in general, are too aware of their weaknesses and not enough of their strengths," Maëlle says. "They spend their careers analyzing everything they don't know how to do to. Women explain why they shouldn't raise their hand, and when they ask a question, they spend their time excusing themselves—'I'm not sure I heard that right...' No, if you are at the table, it is because you are considered to be in your place, and if you ask a really stupid question, I'll tell you."

Among the largest challenges that Frédérique Dame had to face was conquering her own demons—always wanting to be perfect, to do more, hesitating before applying for dream jobs out of fear of not being good enough and not reconciling her ambitions with her potential personal projects. "I'm constantly working on my perfectionism, and I try to keep convincing myself that it is better to advance than to wait for everything to be absolutely perfect, because it never will be." Done is better than perfect, the saying goes. Frédérique says, "When I sent an email, I spent much more time than necessary. It was a way to psychologically delay any refusal, or to protect myself from being too brilliant and having everything that I wanted right away. Ever since I became aware of this 'flaw,' I try to do things as quickly as possible—the no comes in faster, but so does the yes. As a result, I have picked up a momentum I never had before."

When Frédérique was a student, she dreamed about going to the United States. Once she graduated, she sent her resumé to Motorola and other telecom companies, but never got an answer. Skillfully, she decided to contact her school alumni who had settled in the United States and sent an email with the subject line, "New graduate in distress." She got a number of answers inviting her to come for interviews and to participate in the Santa Clara job fair. Frédérique was 23 at the time, and she had never taken a long-haul flight. A bit intimidated, she asked her father to go with her. "We stayed in a motel in Palo Alto. Once on Highway 101, I started to panic and ask myself what I was doing there. I calmed myself down by saying, 'You can't do that to your dad. We'll see how it goes tomorrow, after a good night's sleep.' What happened at that moment demonstrated what would be a strength for my entire career, that ability to reason and coach myself mentally. I calmed my own panic. I also learned to conquer my shyness. After my preparatory class, I realized that shyness cut me off from the world I wanted to join. I said to myself that if I didn't overcome that inhibition, I would never amount to anything. When you push your own limits, you realize that it isn't so bad. I would never had done public speaking before."

Frédérique arrived in the United States in May 2000. There was no LinkedIn, Facebook, Skype, or smartphones. Going abroad at the time was still like free falling, while today we've got a parachute. Today, we have more information than ever to succeed. We can see who knows who, who invests in what, etc. Frédérique had to make a place for herself in the ecosystem without the help of any of today's social networks. It was just when the first Silicon Valley Internet bubble burst that Frédérique found herself on the job market, thanks to the first company that had hired her. Every morning, she would use Ryze.com and Yahoo! Groups to meet new professional contacts. "There weren't the means we have today, but I used what I had. As soon as you start making an excuse, you are setting yourself up for failure. If you say the economy is bad, you'll never find a job." For seven years, being dependent on having a visa to work was very hard, because if she were fired, she may have had to return to France. Every time she changed companies, she had to start from zero again and ask for a green card. Expatriation includes risk taking at its highest level. Nobody was waiting for her. "I wasn't a typical engineer because I didn't code. I was a French woman in tech and I didn't graduate from an American university (nobody knew about the school I attended). People didn't know how to classify me. I always had to justify and prove myself, doing two times more to be accepted. At Ubisoft, they accepted me right away. There was an alignment between our professional and personal values that just increased as the interviews proceeded. It was the same with Uber. It went very quickly. I was hired in ten days. Travis Kalanick said, 'Everything is done manually. We need to automate the driver experience.' I accepted the job. When you find a fit with someone and you don't have to keep proving your value, its magical."

Frédérique's experience is proof that self-confidence is like a muscle. It's not because you don't have any at a given time that you won't ever have any. Fany Pechiodat, the founder of My Little Paris, is very familiar with fear. For her, you need to master it. It will not go away, so it is better to tame it and learn to live with it rather than trying to avoid it, because every time you refuse to confront it, fear grows. Fany panics when it comes to speaking in public. Her solution to face this fear is to bring along her associate Bruno, who can take over if she panics too much. There are always solutions. You need to be creative. Founding your own business could allow you to say no to everything you don't want to do.

Clémentine Piazza took a huge risk when she founded her startup InMemori by investing all of her savings in it. She wasn't afraid of the financial risk, which is rather rare among women. What she did need before she launched, however, was to confirm the usefulness of her service, and that is why she went into the field. "When I met families, I understood that our service answered a real need and I had the financial means to start it and remain fully independent. I was ready to launch, without any major worries. Indeed, I always thought that when you are lucky enough to have an education, that you can pretty much find work if you need it. We need to put more value on that. For me, your education, not your career, represents choice and security. I don't think you can wipe out your fears, but you can be aware of them, which is already fantastic. My technique is to turn up the volume on my fears in order to see what I really am afraid of. In the end, there's not much I really fear. It's not that I have fewer doubts than others. I don't know if I'm going to succeed. But I do want to see if I can."

Money is key for all entrepreneurs who are setting out. It is the second major reason startups fail, as a recent study done by *CB Insights* shows. "Money should never be a reason for fear," says Hélène Duval, founder of YUJ. "You should dare to take risks and tell yourself that your life is an extraordinary experience. There is never a day that is the same, and if only to experience that, it is wonderful. I don't believe there is a school for entrepreneurs, nor do I believe in duplicating recipes. You need to be yourself, and not be afraid to fall down. Every day, I say that perhaps all this will stop, but it's positive. I will have done it."

When Rachel Delacour and her husband founded BIME Analytics, their competition was in Silicon Valley. They really had to create an illusion of being there. They communicated entirely in English, and they brought in young English-speaking people to help them. Rachel spent one week a month in California meeting clients, participating in startup competitions, working on American-style pitching, not so much to win the prizes but because she needed visibility and credibility for her business. "I put myself in terribly uncomfortable situations, at a crazy emotional cost. I wasn't listening to myself. If you start listening to yourself, you stay at home. I thank myself for being so blind to fears because today I am very much at ease in a number of areas." Every time Rachel did this kind of exercise, her team's motivation doubled. Rachel is naturally brave, and never hesitated to use the Internet, notably via LinkedIn, to contact people that interested her and tell them about her project. "I always said, 'What risk are you taking through your screen?' It is so hard to stand out. If you don't do your own promotion, who will? Entrepreneurs need to understand that."

Being bold has a thousand faces. It is that boost in momentum that will allow you to take your projects further, to reach the edges of your dreams, and to go beyond. It is also freedom's best friend, and a passport for success, even if you path is completely off the beaten track.

Maïa Baudelaire is married to Benoist Grossmann, one of the best-known figures in capital risk in Paris with the firm IdInvest, but she is not "his wife." She has an astonishing life, which stems from being bold and authentic. Maïa was born in Paris, but at three months, she moved to Morocco with her parents. She lived there for eleven years. Her mother was a midwife and her father an agricultural engineer working for the French government, helping developing countries become self-sufficient. He made his career in the World Bank and Maïa's mother had to abandon her job to follow him, but she was a strong-headed woman, who more or less started coaching her husband's career. Having grown up living internationally, born from two generations of expatriates, Maïa learned to be very flexible and adaptable, to build new friendships, to learn languages (she is trilingual), to discover new cultures. This taste for discovery also guided her career. Maïa had a lot of fun in high school in Rome, but she didn't work at all and didn't graduate. Her studies ended up being eclectic and with an American degree in nutrition and a master's degree in economics, she had a hard time attracting headhunters in France. One day, she boldly wrote a letter to the CEO of Unilever. After an interview with him, he confirmed his interest and asked the HR manager to see her. The latter, who only hired people with traditional business school profiles, looked down on her, pointed out the holes in her resumé and told her there wasn't a job for her in the company. When Maïa got out of that interview, she called the CEO and said she didn't understand, she had gone to be hired. And the HR manager ended up hiring her.

Maïa wasn't full of self-confidence, as her path was an unusual one, but this deficit in self-confidence was counterbalanced by a tendency toward leadership that came from her family, which had a matriarchal model. She had grown up with examples of women, including her mother and her grandmother, that could be qualified as real adventurers. For three years, she volunteered in Asia helping drug addicts and prostitutes. When the director of the center died, she took over the community without a second thought. One day, Maïa swam across the Strait of Messina, not even knowing if she could do it. "Sometimes, you can push beyond your own limits without planning to do so. You lock up the fear. I hate speaking in public. At Unilever, I spent my time talking in front of large audiences and throwing up behind the scenes. People told me I looked perfectly calm. Seeing my husband work in venture capital, I said to myself, 'Why not try to use something I have inside me?' I founded my business in 2015, focused on my passion for nutrition. I had breast cancer and it was a first trigger, but not enough for me to make the jump. Every day is precious. I had wanted to start my business for a long time, but I didn't have enough confidence in myself. A work psychologist told me, 'You're not doing it because you are afraid, but afraid of what?' Of failure and what others would think. We worked on that and, one morning, I woke up and said, 'I'm going to do it.' What is extraordinary is that once the fear is gone, you wake up to an infinite horizon."

Learn to say yes

Wisdom is to have dreams big enough not to lose sight when we pursue them.

—Oscar Wilde

Sometimes what shows up is different than the plans we make in our heads and yet could have a positive long-term impact. In the beginning of 2012, I was approached by the British government (directly by Prime Minister James Cameron's cabinet) to move LeWeb to London for the summer Olympic Games. There was no way I was going to move the Paris December event to June in London. That said, in the matter of a few hours we made the decision to organize a second event in London in June 2012, in addition to the one in Paris. My only condition was that they find us a place to do it in London, a place that met my standards. If I did a LeWeb in London, it couldn't be a sub-product of the one in Paris. It was a major challenge, and having two events was a huge risk. We needed to find sponsors without any certainty about the number of participants, and we needed to mobilize teams. But we even did it twice, with the second edition taking place in 2013. I set up the London event with my Paris teams. We took everyone along on the adventure. My head of design even took an accelerated English class, surprising us all. Organizing LeWeb in London gave us an opportunity to make a difference, to get out of our comfort zone, and to broaden the business.

LeWeb didn't have employees, but a dream team of independent contractors. I only wanted people who were responsible for what they were doing, who were fully in charge. While others didn't know how to rebound using the success of the conference, Sibylle de Villeneuve managed to capitalize on it without cannibalizing it. I met Sibylle in 1999 for RapidSite, for which she handled press relations within an agency named Singapore. She was there with us in front row seats during the first Internet bubble that was an incredible tidal wave of energy and projects. When we put together LeWeb, naturally she was the one to continue to work on building our influence. Sibylle gave so much, getting involved in ways that went way beyond her assignment on paper. She dared to pick up challenges, such as speaking English, which was a nightmare for her, but I knew she would give it her all and it wouldn't be a problem. Our collaboration was based on trust and commitment. The way Sibylle took LeWeb to be an opportunity to drive her own career forward was deeply intelligent. She was very close to the clients, but always under the banner of LeWeb. When in

January 2013 she created her own agency, Raoul, she recuperated everything she had accomplished. "I realized that taking care of LeWeb for ten years had been a springboard, my professional starting point. It was a major turning point in my life, my years of preparatory class, if you will. Géraldine had delegated communications to me and it had to be well managed. It had to be perfect. There was pressure, but also a framework of autonomy and trust. Not disappointing them was more important than being tired. We were an extremely small team, where each person had their private preserve, and everything worked smoothly. It was this excellence found in everyone at LeWeb that keeps bringing opportunities to me today. I draw great strength from perseverance and from the respect I get from my clients."

She was able to build a long-term network by being bold and not alienating herself. I benefited from the same when I went looking for people to support me in building The Refiners. They all showed up.

The success of a product stems from a combination of work and opportunities that you grab. "I do not believe in luck," Isabelle Bordry says. "There are opportunities you take or don't. It's said that in competitive examinations, 25 percent depends on your physical condition, 25 percent on luck, and 50 percent on work, so it is work that counts above all." Be a yes girl, trust in serendipity, and you will go so much further than you imagine.

The way in which Fleur Pellerin reinvented a career in the private sector after a first life as a high-level public servant and politician is a superb illustration of the art of seizing opportunities on the fly. Fleur held three consecutive positions in the government, all the while keeping in mind that politics is tough, requires a lot of personal commitment, can be violent, and does not necessarily recognize you. You are constantly in an ejector seat. She was dismissed from her position under unusual circumstances, while she was in the process of defending a law before the senate. Fortunately, she is extremely resilient. "I left for California. When I came back, I was in great physical shape and I turned the page quickly. I had a lot of friends who had been members of the government and who had a lot harder time grieving over that period, because they had been in politics for a long time and had never had another profession. It was very reassuring to know that I had a profession and I knew how to do other things. I'm not at all inclined to rehashing things. It is a shock to find yourself back in a normal life, but how you handle it depends on your capacity to keep your feet on the ground. I never considered that people were my lackeys. I was always pragmatic, and I didn't think it was strange to be taking the metro again. I had an incredible luxury, since I had been a civil servant, and I returned to my job at the revenue court, where I had started out, all the while knowing that I wouldn't stay there long. It's a job I had done for over ten years and I had pretty much exhausted what it had to offer, so I couldn't image staying long." She considered joining the private sector, but didn't really know where. Headhunters offered her jobs that traditionally go to former ministers, but they were all positions in which she would have had a boss, and that didn't attract her. Then one day, she got an offer to lead a capital risk management company. She refused, but a seed had been planted in her mind.

A succession of coincidences led her to found Korelya Capital. Fleur was born in Korea. She was adopted and had never returned to her country of birth until she was a minister in the French government. When she went as a member of the government, she received a frenzied welcome. The Koreans considered her to be one of their own, even though she was not at all bicultural. When she left the government, she returned to Korea for the first time with a little time for herself. She figured that it would be unfortunate to not take advantage of the special status she had there. The founders of Naver, the first Korean Internet portal, were beginning to contemplate a European strategy and let her know they'd like to work with her. "I told them that if they wanted to understand the European ecosystem, the first thing to do was to invest and see what European entrepreneurs were made of. They asked how much I would need. I said, '100 million.' They accepted. I raised 100 million in one day. I hadn't gone there with the idea of creating my own business. When I got home, I wondered what I was going to do. It took a few months, as it is rather complicated to put together a capital risk business in terms of regulations and administration. I spent all summer working with attorneys to structure an investment vehicle, to put together a team and to find offices.

"I jumped in, even though I saw my father start a business in the 1980s, and for me founding a business represented an enormous risk and responsibility to the family, with huge amounts of stress. My father sold high-tech medical research equipment, a very procyclical activity. He started his business in 1987, just before the economic crisis, which hit him head on because he was heavily dependent on big hospitals and university centers, and my mother was not working. I remember when he came back from the bank that had refused him a loan. Everything depended on my father, who was the only one to bring money home. My parents had just adopted my little sister and bought a house that had been mortgaged. For me, it was more of a traumatic memory, and perhaps unconsciously that is why I chose to be a public servant first. And yet, the only thing I said to myself when I was creating Korelya was, 'Either you keep looking for a job where you'll have a boss (when I was at a time in my life when I did not want anyone to tell me what to do), or risk it now, knowing it's a bit like the last time you can do it.' I was in my forties. I think It's a lot harder, when you've never done it before, to start at age 50, once the kids are grown up. I imagined it was the only time I would have the energy, the opportunity, and an alignment of planets that probably would not come around a second time." Fleur recognized that she was in a particularly favorable context, where risk-taking was measured. She chose to resign from the public service when her status would have allowed her time off for eight years, after which she would have had the choice to resign or to return to the public service. It was a huge safety net, but she did not feel comfortable taking it in view of her Korean investors and the people she had recruited. Symbolically, it was very important for her to step down and make a 100 percent commitment to this entrepreneurial venture.

Fleur partnered with a former classmate, who had 20 years of experience in the merger and acquisition business, in London and the United States. They would never have imagined that one day they would work together. The way in which the work is organized within the fund is quite similar to what Fleur had set up in the office, around a small team that was very tight. "I did not experience huge culture shock in terms of organization and pace of work. There are ten of us (in a cabinet, there are 10 to 15 people), I travel a lot, I found a balance for my family. My quality of life has improved significantly. My daughter is delighted. I had not had a vacation for five years, and now we can go on vacation together." Now Fleur can take her daughter to the doctor.

Don't think too much

> *In all that one undertakes, one must give two-thirds to reason, and the other third to chance. Increase the first fraction, and you will lack courage. Increase the second, you will be reckless.*
>
> —Napoleon Bonaparte

Mike Arrington, who created *TechCrunch*, nicknamed me Napoleon after seeing how LeWeb grew and how I managed the event and my teams. At The Refiners, business partners baptized me "Patton" when we began working together, probably because of my taste for quick and effective execution. General George S. Patton said, "A good plan violently executed now is better than a perfect plan executed next week." Does one necessarily have to be a male military leader in order to lead effectively? The following examples should convince you otherwise.

In leading the Sigfox Foundation, Marion Moreau asks others for their opinions and of course has moments of doubt, like everyone, and yet she charges forward. "I'm a fight-to-the-finish kind of person, especially when it comes to defending a cause. You shouldn't think too much. By having been involved in the beginning of the wave of new technologies means that I ask a lot fewer questions. We needed to figure everything out, not knowing how life-changing lines of code would prove. It is a revolution and we are in the process of following along, carried by a powerful impetus."

The capacity to allow yourself to be carried by the flow of circumstances and to learn on the job is a quality seen in Roxanne Varza, who I interviewed on January 3, 2018. She was born in Palo

Alto to parents who had immigrated to the United States at the time of the Iranian revolution, and she spent most of her life there. Attracted by France, she decided to do her Master's degree there. In 2009, after working with startups in Silicon Valley that wanted to export to Europe, she moved back to France. Seeing that a lot of fascinating things were occurring in France and that nobody knew about them, she decided to promote the initiatives she found exciting. First, she did so through a personal blog, and then on *TechCrunch*, and through the network Girls In Tech. Today, she heads up Station F, a giant startup campus created by the French billionaire businessman Xavier Niel. Roxanne has always approached what she was doing with creativity, always succeeded in creating her legitimacy right from the start, and has always taken clear stands. The first day she wrote for *TechCrunch*, she was afraid. "That was the moment I felt the least legitimate in my entire career. I really wanted to do it, but I didn't think I was at all credible writing in French about tech. I was lucky to be surrounded by a good support system." She dared to take risks and put herself in uncomfortable situations. "Often, I love the sound of a project when someone talks to me about it, I say yes, and I think about it afterwards. That is what happened with Station F. With time, you accept that you will never perfectly master all the subjects and that there is no better way to learn than in the field." That is how she found herself working as a construction entrepreneur, supervising the renovation of the huge Halle Freyssinet, transforming it from a former train station into an ultra-modern center designed to house 1,000 startups.

"Don't ask too many questions. There comes a time you just need to dive in and learn to swim afterwards," says Mathilde Thomas. The crazy experience she had with Caudalie is proof that you can do it. "I was under the impression that there were two roads in front of us, and that we always took the hardest, the most complicated. I see it because my competitors often choose the easiest solutions," she adds. During her last year at business school, Mathilde absolutely wanted to work in cosmetics and perfumes. She had done all of her internships in companies in the perfume capital of Grasse, working with raw material suppliers. Her companion, who attended another business school, wanted to start a company. One fine weekend in October 1993, right in the middle of the grape harvest, Mathilde and Bertrand found themselves in vineyards belonging to Mathilde's parents and met Professor Vercauteren from the Bordeaux faculty of pharmaceutical science. They gave him a tour of the Smith Haut-Lafitte estate. He said he found the wine very good, but they were throwing away the most noble part of the plant. He told them about the virtues of grape seeds, explaining that they contained polyphenols that were ten thousand times more powerful than vitamin E to neutralize free radicals. He was referring to the same free radicals that cause fruit to brown, that rust cars, turn butter rancid, and that are responsible for four out of every five human wrinkle. Polyphenols improve blood circulation and reduce the sensation of heavy legs as well.

Mathilde and Bertrand's hearts both skipped a beat. The next day, they showed up at the Bordeaux faculty of pharmaceutical sciences, in Professor Vercauteren's office, to get the low-down on his discoveries. They asked why nobody was using these famous polyphenols, and he explained that they were extremely unstable and when you extract them from the seeds and add them as is to a cream, they turn the latter a very red wine-like color and lose their effectiveness. It was lucky then that the professor was in the process of filing a patent for a process that stabilized the polyphenols. They decide to become associates and founded the limited company Caudalie in 1994.

They were young, students, and naïve. Their first market studies taught them at there were already 800 brands distributed in pharmacies, that the market was saturated, and that these products have too high an added value to be appropriate for retail distribution. They saw the hurdles but were convinced they had an extraordinary patent in their hands, so they launched the company. Everyone they knew advised them to go work for L'Oréal, to learn first, except for Mathilde's father, who encouraged them to go for it. "There's no point playing office politics in a large company. Try, and you'll see if it works." As a couple, they were very complementary and had been in the habit of working together since their early years of study. They don't question their decision. The distribution of roles occurred naturally—Mathilde in product development, brand design management, and communication, and Bertrand for all the rest—organization, commercialization and finance. Mathilde created her first three formulas by figuring things out, learning a new profession. "When you are an entrepreneur, you are completely reckless. We tried to make ourselves look older. At twenty-three and just out of school, I borrowed my mother's suits, wearing jackets with shoulder pads, while Bertrand wore ties so we would look older than we were. Not only did we look young, but we really didn't know how to do anything. When we went to see the banks to tell them we were going to launch a brand that would make grape-seed-based creams..., well, we saw a lot of them before any accepted to front 50,000 francs for Caudalie."

The brand grew little by little, from pharmacy to pharmacy, until it became known worldwide. Today, Caudalie sells a third of its products in France, a third in Europe, and the final third in the Americas and Asia. The small family business continues to build its success among the mastodons in the sector, and they reinvent themselves constantly. Had they asked themselves a thousand questions ahead of time instead of following their enthusiasm, Mathilde and Bertrand would not have accomplished any of that.

Whether founding a business or having a child, if you wait for the perfect time, you run the risk of never taking action. "You need to go for it, otherwise you never do it," says Marion Carrette, the founder of OuiCar. "You always find a good excuse. When I sold my first business, I went back to a day job and we had our first child. For the second, it was much more complicated. I felt guilty that I couldn't organize the same maternity leave and I kept putting it off. We need to stop asking so many questions." Projecting into the future does nothing; what counts is managing the moment.

"I never thought 'What am I going to do in three years?' I just did it," says Helen Bouygues. "In France, women say, 'I want three children, so I can't travel.' We project too much, and we are not enough in the reality of the present moment. It is very French to limit your options. My point of view is that we don't know what is going to happen, but that if you want to open up intellectually, you should not become too much of a specialist. I don't mean be a dabbler. You need to create situations that can become springboards to something else. Nobody can dictate the right path. If there is one thing to choose consciously for yourself, it is liberty and independence. I love the choice of not being a victim."

Trust yourself, have a direction, but not an outcome, and above all, have values. It took me some time to stop projecting myself into the future. For example, when you sell a business, part of the earnout is linked to projections. An earnout is a contractual provision stating that the seller of a business will receive additional compensation in the future. But it has never turns out the way you imagine it will. We need to stop reasoning in terms of earnout.

Persevere

> *Things must flow naturally, and if a rock blocks your path, you must push it out of the way, or bypass it, or pierce it—that's the natural flow.*
>
> — the river

A career (just like personal life, for that matter) is not always a bed of roses. You will encounter pitfalls along the way, no matter what. And it is just as well. Because the pitfalls allow you to move towards being the best possible you more than the easy successes will.

Entrepreneurship is trendy now. Startupers are today's heroes, haloed in the glory of disruptive innovation. But what we forget all too often is that Rome was not built in a day. Neither were Spotify or Airbnb. Founding a business, bringing it to life, and leading it to success is hard work. It is often a path scattered with both social and material sacrifice. When we founded our first business as a couple, I had to ask for parental backing to rent an apartment.

Rachel Delacour's fine path didn't unfold without suffering. "Today, people are talking a lot about startups, but founding a startup is a marathon you run at double full throttle. There are plenty of new entrepreneurs who think that everything will unfold like it did for

Facebook. People need to think of it like a vocation. Financially, it's tough. When you are 25 or 30 years old, your friends all have rising careers, are getting married, are going on dream trips. I had to go live with my in-laws the year all my friends were getting married. Socially, it was also hard. Nobody said, 'I'd love to be in your shoes.' Sometimes, it is hard to keep the faith, but I always did, thankfully."

Rania Balkahia might have a strong personality, knowing what she wants and where she is going, but she is the first to admit that being an entrepreneur is not always easy. "I worked three times more, because I countered inexperience with work. It's hard not to be paid. To manage everything at the same time, I would go to bed after midnight. You have to be happy doing what you are doing. You build the steps year after year, and you grow. Nobody told me that building a business could take between five and ten years." When she runs, Rania is a great sprinter. When she realized that her entrepreneurial project would require more endurance than she had anticipated, she trained and then ran three marathons to learn about long-term hard effort.

For Hélène Duval, you need to accept to filter what's around you. "You are no longer the available friend or the mom who has time to talk after school. It's my dark side—I can't make everyone happy. My priority is my family and the success of this venture. Your centers of interest change enormously. I have less and less time to lose." The life of an entrepreneur is difficult when it is hard to share it with others. Success itself can also be complicated to experience when those around you feel left behind, out of the loop, or jealous. Your family, your spouse and your friends could provide support, or perhaps they won't."

Entrepreneurship involves complete investment. That does not mean, as we have seen, that you cannot reconcile it with a family life or whatever you need to flourish. But an entrepreneur cannot be separated from her creation. To cite Céline Lazorthes, "When there is a production incident, it is impossible for me not to be on deck. The business is my baby and I need to take good care of it. You can't let your own house burn down." She adds that she would not for a moment go through the throes of building a new company. "What is hard, is making things work. When things are working, it's easy to accelerate them. To be an entrepreneur, you don't need to be very intelligent, but you do need to be very courageous. You need to have good resistance to suffering. I have a very sensitive nature, but I am able to fight for a long time."

When Stéphanie Hospital decided to found her investment fund, she understood quickly that it was much harder than she had imagined. People didn't take her seriously, because she came from the corporate world and she didn't have any of the expected experience. She needed three years to get there. "I had to face obstacles. I wasn't from the world of finance and I had never raised funding. I had mostly been on the side of people who were asked for money. I had to learn to ask. I had an excellent contact with the businessman Jean-Marie Messier. When I told him I wanted to create a platform fund, he said he was willing to do it with me. He trusted me and believed in this project from the first minute. None of my friends in investment could believe it, and that was complicated. Becoming an entrepreneur is a heavy burden personally because you only ever do that. It is the contrary of cushy jobs."

An entrepreneur must know how to listen to advice, collate all the good or bad feedback, and not be shot down when you realize it is time to pivot. The whole art of entrepreneurial perseverance is to build from the opinions of others, to evaluate the situation and say, "What I tried does not work. It is not the end of the world. We had a bad customers feedback, so now, what are we going to change?" This is where it is particularly interesting to zoom out and return to your vision. Conversely, good customer feedback does not mean that the moment has come to rest on your laurels. Nothing is ever certain. There will be times when luck and the serendipity of the meetings will carry you, and you must know how to recognize that. But it is not because something has gone well that it will always be so thereafter. Move forward without being defeated by the pitfalls, but by building an experience.

When you start a new business, you start from scratch. This was the case when I started The Refiners, but also for LeWeb. Every January, I picked up my pilgrim's staff to visit our partners. The idea was always to provide good content for conferences. We were very adamant that sponsors were not buying a place on stage. People were not there to hear the sponsors. Always build, and never consider that it is earned. There is never a fixed horizon in the creation of a product. We must constantly reiterate and always keep our eyes on the mission we want to accomplish.

Corinne Vigreux, the co-founder of TomTom, has had a beautiful 25-year-long entrepreneurial story. And like all beautiful stories, it is rich in twists and courage. Corinne started her career in a small, innovative British company called Psion, one of the first companies to manufacture personal digital assistants. In England in the late 1980s, Corinne discovered a very dynamic entrepreneurial environment, where everything was possible. Very quickly, she took on more and more responsibilities, until she became global export manager, and fell in love with her Dutch distributor, who she decided to follow to the Netherlands. After a first inconclusive Dutch work experience, her husband introduced her to two engineers who were starting a business project developing software to read electrical meters. She joined them and the TomTom adventure began. She transformed the company from BtoB to BtoC. It was when they embarked on mapping for personal digital assistants that their success began. They became leaders in software production for this type of product. Corinne developed an international distribution network. In the late 1990s, they decided to market a complete product for the end consumer, going from two to forty million in sales. Corinne's husband, who had become director of Psion England, joined them in 2001 and they dived into hardware (the famous TomTom). Everyone said, "You are completely crazy, you are software publishers. It will never work, nobody will buy this product." They produced 200,000 GPS units with the idea of the stock lasting a year, and they sold it off in three months. From 40 million sales, they increased to 1.8 billion in five years. They went public in 2005. In 2008, they began to diversify, notably acquiring their TeleAtlas cartographer for about $3 billion.

This was when Google started mapping and decided to offer free navigation on phones. All this happened at the same time. They did panic a little. The company, which had already pivoted several times, was forced to turn around again. "We had to be very resilient in the face of this brutal disruption. We had been growing, for years we had not been able to supply the demand, and suddenly it is as if we were slamming on the brakes. We had difficult decisions to make and continued to invest in research and development when we needed to restructure and reorganize." Today, TomTom is a much more diversified company than before, with, in addition to the general public division, a telematic division, a cartography division, and an automobile division. The company is in the process of transitioning to software development, because the navigation products that allowed it to grow are a shrinking market, even though the company still sells 3 million units a year (to date, TomTom has sold 90 million GPS systems).

Successive transitions went well, the business was profitable, but it was not painless. The hardest thing for Corinne were the layoffs during restructuring. "It's important for me to always let people go with respect, recognizing their value and contribution. The way I managed to overcome the pain of separating myself from people was to say that TomTom was a good school for them. They learned a lot from us, we gave them responsibilities, and in general they find a job fairly quickly."

To those who decide to start a business, Corinne likes to say that entrepreneurship is not a lifestyle. Being an entrepreneur means taking risks, identifying problems and making sure you use the best technologies to solve them. It is an activity that takes a lot of space in our lives. We do not talk about a balance between professional and personal life, because the two merge. The entrepreneurial project is central, hence the importance of guiding your choices to ensure that you enjoy it. Making a difference gives you a fantastic amount of energy. "I love it when I am told that our products have saved thousands of marriages as couples don't argue over what road to take," Corinne adds.

Know when to let go

It is impossible to live without failing at something, unless you live so cautiously that you might as well have not lived at all – in which case, you fail by default.

— J.K. Rowling

You need to ensure that your perseverance does not become stubbornness. Here too, an outside perspective can be precious. Marion Carrette founded Zilok in 2007, before the explosion of collaborative consumer platforms. Ahead of the curve, she had to be very patient and asked Marc Simoncini to warn her if he thought she was pushing forward uselessly. Patience also means taking the time to take care of your primary market and have a product that works without a hitch before looking to deploy internationally. This she learned because Zilok wanted to expand to the United Kingdom and the United States too early on. In the end, the long years of work on Zilok allowed her to learn a lot and to build expertise, on which she was able to capitalize to create OuiCar successfully.

Mathilde Thomas, the co-founder of Caudalie, gives the same advice. "One of the keys is to focus and not to go off in every direction. Focus on a country or a product and dig deep before moving on. Of all the mistakes we've made, the biggest has perhaps been to go too far too fast. We opened a beautiful vinotherapy spa on the family property, which gave us a global spotlight from one day to the next, and as a result we were asked to distribute to Japan, the United States, and Australia. We said yes to everything. We flew around the world in economy class and slept on couches of expatriate friends on the other side of the world (for lack of budget). We were exhausted. We opened to other countries without realizing that we had to create a team and come back five times a year for meetings. We used up our strength, especially at the beginning. Instead of adopting a snowball or snail strategy, starting in France then opening to Italy, Germany, etc., we went everywhere. I do not advise doing that. First, you need to have a strong organization and be strong at home."

In 1999, Loïc and I sold our business RapidSite to Nicolas Dufourcq, who was CEO of Wanadoo (France Telecom). At the same time, we sold B2L to the Omnicom BBDO group. We were 27 years old and had two children. It was an incredible turning point, something that had an enormous impact on the rest of our entrepreneurial life. There never was any question about stopping. We had been bitten by the entrepreneurial bug. So, we decided to build what today we would call a "startup studio" called Business

Pace. The idea was to reinvest a large portion of our money and continue having ambitious projects. We created and raised funds for a number of companies, with the idea of integrating the entire value chain. We had in-house legal, human resources, finance, marketing and engineers, which represented a core team of about ten people. We started the projects and then we found teams to implement them. But I think there is a very strong principle in entrepreneurship that if it's too early, it cannot work. A number of our projects were ahead of the market and could not find their product-market fit because at that time, they did not solve a problem identified by the market. We burned a lot of personal money but learned a lot. This experience was very constructive. I really understood that when a market was not ready, you can have an excellent idea, but it will not find its audience. We still see it today with companies that are very successful when the same ideas fell completely flat five or six years ago. The key question is "What is the problem we solve?" Business Pace also allowed us to embark on the Ublog adventure. In all, the startup studio survived fewer than three years. You need to know when to cut things off. You need to realize when it is not working.

You have to be very rational, to listen carefully to those around you, while having convictions. When you say to yourself, "I really did everything that seems to me to be reasonable enough to make my project work," it's time to give up. Be careful not to hold on to stubbornness or pride for fear of losing face. A successful failure will not be badly judged. It is okay to be wrong, to iterate, to experiment, even if it leads you to pivot very far from the initial project. But you must also know how to say, "Stop." Ask yourself if you have viewed the question from all sides. Get advice. Ask questions shamelessly, without too much affect. You need to give it everything you've got, but if you see that the product does not find its customers or that the passion disappears, it is better to let go.

It is important to safeguard your strength. The burden is heavy when you have employees and people who rely on you, but it is not doing them any good to keep a company running for another six months if it has to shut down sooner than that. If you destroy your health, you will not be a good manager. You have to know your limits.

Learn how to care for yourself. Fanny Bouton, the founder of 1000110 and the organizer of the Fanny's Party since 2003, does just that. "I am a queen when it comes to going for a massage day. I disappear. As I program tweets ahead of time, everyone thinks that I do not stop." This allows her to last better over time, so she does not reach a breaking point.

Also remember to celebrate the victories encountered along the way—even the small ones! Alice Guilhon, dean of SKEMA Business School, had her greatest victory on a tennis court when she was 14 years old; the newspapers called her "the Mozart of tennis." Her father had never traveled to see her play, except that day. She had pushed so hard that she could not walk. And yet, she just said, "That's done," and was already thinking about the next step. Today, she knows how important it is to take advantage of moments of success and pause.

When you push too far, your body will be quick to call you to order. Helen Bouygues had grown her company to a critical size, beyond which she realized she could no longer manage it. "You can manage four or five teams at the same time, not more. I had a team of consultants who, on average, had two or three children each. If one day I did not bring in business, what would become of their families? Either I had to find an associate, or reduce my scope, or sell out. A serious bout of sciatica forced me to take two weeks off. I did not find anyone with the same values or the same working standards as me to associate with. So, I joined a large consulting firm."

Selling your company is not a neutral act. It is like separating from your "baby," but it can be a great experience. For Rachel Delacour, it was a moment of great excitement, and the beginning of new opportunities. "It felt like shedding bags of bricks I didn't want to be carrying. For 18 months I felt much lighter, but an inkling that something was missing finally settled in, a desire to start over again. Today, I'm happy to have more time for myself, but also to give back to the ecosystem. I asked Zendesk to reduce my time to 70 percent so I could give 30 percent of my time to France Digitale, a leading French association committed to growing the French tech ecosystem with prominent members from both the venture capital and the entrepreneurial world. Shortly after our interview, Rachel took over the co-presidency of France Digitale, and is working to make more space for women in the association's actions, for example by organizing "women's office hours."

Chapter 4

Leaders

I believe deeply in female leadership. When a woman is in the right position, nothing will stop her, because she is courageous, lucid, and if meaning leads her, she will not stop on the way. That is why I hire women.
—Clémentine Piazza, founder of InMemori

Is there a specifically female management approach? Do men and women in positions of responsibility cultivate the same leadership style? These questions remain unanswered, but when Fany Pechiodat showed us her little office on the top floor under the rooftops on the premises of My Little Paris, she said, "This is a real woman's office. A man would have torn down the walls to make it bigger." I saw some truth in her words. Of all the women I met to write this book, I found little attachment to symbols of apparent power, and egos stepping aside to make room for the needs of the overall project.

I see a complementary approach to leadership between men and women. Female leaders will bring something different to management than men. It seems to me that women tend to listen more than speaking at all costs. The educator and businessman Stephen R. Covey says, "Most people do not listen with the intent to understand; they listen with the intent to reply." Could this be a male issue? I personally place a high priority on dialogue. It is better to have an open, calm discussion than to sweep the dust under the rug.

In 2014, Isabelle Bordry was leading the Paris Region European election list for the Nous Citoyens party. She has fond memories of the experience as a woman politician, other than the campaign fatigue, and she encourages other women to join politics. "It's a wonderful experience to fight for ideas. Women can get a lot from it, because they are often less in a confrontational mode and more inclined to consensus, which makes it easier to go farther, better. There is a difference in the relationship to power. A woman wants power for an outcome that is not only about being in the limelight. We are more in a consensual and collective dimension, less drawn to confrontation and competition. Female management leaves more room for listening. The fact that there are more women in strategic positions contributes to spreading this kind of approach."

For Frédérique Dame, being French in the United States means being different by default. "When you work in a culture that is not your own, you are automatically categorized as intrinsically different. It could have been hard, but I turned this to my advantage and I have always cultivated this difference. After all, no matter our culture, we are all different. As a result, I define myself by my own standards, not in reference to others. I only compete with myself. When I was a team leader for Uber, the qualities that came to the surface were that I was kind, calming and altruistic, while also being single-minded and determined. Kindness is a character trait that could seem to be devoid of ambition, but it suits me and allowed me to develop trust with my team members. If I succeed alone, it is not a victory. You set your ego aside when you are discussing a product, because the product needs to win in the end."

Women, agile leaders

I wake up every morning and think to myself, "How far
can I push the company forward in the next 24 hours?"
—Leah Busque

In an economy that is ever more complex and fluctuating, tomorrow's leaders will need to be more and more agile and to demonstrate soft skills. Agility is the capacity to move and make decisions quickly and with grace. It allows leaders to face today's challenges of volatility, uncertainty, complexity and ambiguity, where change is both inevitable and unforeseeable, and to do so with the distance needed to prepare for the future. For a leader, agility is a mindset that facilitates quick growth and the adoption of key strategies. It helps to adapt to change, to remain resilient during periods of uncertainty, and to learn from all experiences, even failures.

In their Afrimarket entrepreneurial adventure, Rania Belkahia and her cofounder demonstrated significant agility. Their initial idea in 2013 was to target the African diaspora in France, a clientele with little digital presence. The concept was to get African immigrants to send products to their families rather than money. They began by going to Abidjan to develop a network of partners and test the appeal to their target market. The test was conclusive and they decided to run a first pilot in the Ivory Coast. At first, they thought the project was to launch a site, but as they sat in front of Google Analytics watching traffic, they had to face the reality that nothing was happening. They realized they had to reinvent their project. The began by launching the business with their own funding, and once the proof of concept was complete, they raise their first half-million euros, even with so many doors still being closed on Africa at the time, it being perceived as a risky market. The team grew and they opened up to Senegal and Benin. They feel the need for extra funding and begin discussions with Orange, finalizing the second funding in January 2015. This allowed them to begin investing in logistic infrastructures. Working in countries where the latter are lacking, they needed to control the whole supply chain to offer quality service, which meant taking command of logistics. Once they established the systems, they were ready to target their real market, the local market, strengthened by their experiences working with the diaspora. Their goal was to be able to deliver everywhere, including to villages, with the ambition of being a last-mile company.

In July 2016, they raised 10 million euros to really establish themselves in five Francophone West African countries. Their goal was to develop local ecommerce, which today represents 80 percent of their volume. This was no small challenge. They were targeting first buyers online with no credit cards and no addresses, so they had to find alternatives and reinvent everything, placing the African consumer at the center of the model. "We are very attentive to fair pricing, with the idea in mind that an ecosystem represents a distribution of value for everyone," says Rania. "Afrimarket is not a social business, but there are fabulous positive externalities. We are very happy to say that we respect the ecosystem, that we have managed to align the interests of all the shareholders in the chain, including the governments, which are happy to see formal circuits develop. We are the first to have developed express delivery in Africa. Every day, we have to create additional added value with the same budgets and the same teams. Since September 2017, we have had monthly growth of 20 percent. Today, we are truly in a phase a of organic growth, and no longer just optimization. We need to test and learn as we go along. I believe that ideas are like a living matter that evolves based on customer needs. I often advise new entrepreneurs to do a version 0 and to evolve over time." At the beginning, to be able to launch a business, you need to answer the "idea/need" equation, but the answer is only a freeze frame at the given moment of the vision. When you are aware of that, you act like an agile leader.

In 2016, Emily Livorsi wrote an article defining eight characteristics of agile leaders. They set direction, execute and follow through with calculated speed, know how to effectively align resources (especially human resources), inspire others to be better and to accept change, think strategically, understand talent development, and seek personal development.

Agile leaders have a clear idea where they want to go and see the path that will take them there. They are attentive to lighting up the path for others and giving them the keys to be able to embody the company's vision. When important opportunities arise, agile leaders know how to combine quick decision making with careful planning and organization in order to reach the best results. They know how to communicate effectively in order to convince key stakeholders and to engage their team members. Teams working with agile leaders understand what their role is, what the expectations are, and they feel capable of meeting them.

Frédérique Dame's experience at Uber helped her advance toward agile leadership. "Uber is the best experience I had in the Valley during my career. I transformed like never before. It was tough emotionally because the product, the teams and the company were growing so quickly and we had to stay on course, but I was rewarded by my own growth on all levels. My communication style is more direct than ever, just as I know how to adapt to the people I'm talking to. I developed leadership skills on the go because at the pace we were going, we needed to inspire our engineers and to explain the impact of their work on the transport ecosystem, or else we could have lost them to a more competitive offer."

Personally, I have always deeply trusted the people I worked with, both women and men. Agile leaders know how to channel the talents of those around them into the service of the project. They are acutely aware of each person's role and value within the overall organization. Delphine Bellini, today the managing director of the Schiaparelli fashion house, perfectly illustrates this kind of leadership filled with emotional intelligence.

When she was director of development and the general manager of JC de Castelbajac, her mission was to create value around the brand and its reputation, and to support licensed partners with an organizational structure that supported the growth of the brand's influence. This meant structuring and coordinating the teams and partners that surrounded Jean-Charles de Castelbajac. "Today, people talk a lot about participative management. I never worked in any other way and have always involved my teams and my coworkers in the decision-making process. Listening and sharing are key to the success of an entrepreneurial project. This approach federates teams around a vision and strong values, leaning on each person's expertise, developing their talents by motivating them and giving them independence. Showing esteem and trust to your teams helps to build a project calmly and to advance much more quickly. Taking everyone along on the adventure also forges a mindset. Working hand in hand, asking questions, supporting coworkers at all levels, seeing farther—these are elements of an entrepreneurial project. You have to be in action and in anticipation all the time. It is a mindset and you have to be two steps ahead in your strategy and in all aspects of your development.

"I have a very operational approach," she continues. "I learned the different jobs in the fashion and perfume sector in the field, with coworkers. I want to know how things work and to know what I'm talking about, making decisions because I know what impact they will have. I challenge my coworkers because I know that that will help them grow, which will benefit the project. You have to know what people do and who they are. I work with the teams, I listen to them, I accompany them. It is not always easy, but that is how we move forward."

The art of accompanying and listening to people also makes it possible to transform threats into opportunities. "Whether an organization is large or small, internal communication is always an issue. Proximity among coworkers helps to smooth over choppy or irregular communication, and sometimes to seize opportunities and turn around complex situations. I also think there is certainly a more feminine side in this approach, something that is both virtuous and benevolent," Delphine says. "Before entering a conflict, we'll look to see how a complicated situation can be turned into a win-win situation."

Agile leaders know how to pass on their passion to others and help coworkers to reach their own objectives. They also motivate others to embrace change, even when it is difficult. "Strategy is not enough. You have to have a concrete vision share by everyone. Operational implementation is key, including the organization, the processes, talent development, and aligning team members with the company's values. You need to identify the change that is occurring and figure out how to leap in with both feet. You need a lot of flexibility, courage, combativity, along with strong opinions and belief in your intuition. Today, we are living in a world where you need to believe in yourself and not be afraid to fail. Assessing an entrepreneur by their failures is a very American notion. In France, there is the problem of industry compartmentalization, that fortunately is dying out. People often hire others with exactly the same career path and share the same diploma because it is reassuring. I believe that deeply impacts the possibilities for differentiation. Go elsewhere to see how things are being done and keep an open mind. You can learn from ever field and skills transfer is very beneficial in businesses. I often ask my coworkers and partners to go see what the best practices are in other sectors of activity. What leads to success in fashion today is not enough for me. Cultivating an open mind allows us to move mountains. A good entrepreneur should be creative, not only in what she or he produces, but also in her or his management and approach."

Agile leaders have the humility and perspicacity to know that they cannot attack the business's problems alone, so they inspire others to grow alongside them. They find people who like to learn and provide them with opportunities to grow. They also know how to shine the spotlight on others. Delphine Bellini explains, "Success stems from everyone, not just one person. After an accomplishment, when a major threshold has been crossed, I always take the time to bring our teams together to share that small moment of victory and to thank those who deserve it. When people have done particularly good work, I like to highlight it. It is very gratifying for everyone and these are moments of intense joy."

Agile leaders see errors as opportunities for learning. They are benevolent with themselves and balance their quest for personal excellence by understanding that trial and error are part of leadership development. Frédérique Dame accents the importance of resilience. "Everything that is worth it requires a little (or a lot) of effort. Remember that hard times and turns of fortune do not last. They allow you to appreciate the good times, and to know that you are strong. The secret to my resilience has always been the idea that life is a voyage and that the final objective is a moving target. You will always come through, and you can always find something positive in every situation. A refusal can bruise your ego, but that is not the end of the world. See what you can learn from it, and move on to something else."

As she notes, "When you take small risks and fail, it is useful to do a post-mortem analysis. Was there any intuition that I didn't listen to? That doesn't mean you should go ahead with things the next time, but listening to your intuition allows you to be more in tune with who you are. We have a sixth sense. Know how to use it."

"Don't be too hard on yourself," she insists. "I learned that from an athlete who told me, 'When I fail, I give myself 48 hours to take it in, and then I move on to something else.' When you make a mistake, you learn something. But don't beat yourself up over it. Move on. For me, everything in the past belongs to the past, even the successes. Life is in front of you, not behind you. Even success can paralyze you and keep you from more success. The work is changing quickly, and today's success will be nothing more than a line on your resumé tomorrow. Keep up the pace and continue to advance towards your goals, or towards what represents success for you. With a little luck, a win will provide you some room to maneuver to adjust your trajectory to do more of what you love to do. That is a real luxury. The word to remember is freedom."

Frédérique Dame also says, "There are no shortcuts to personal growth. It takes work, tenacity, learning about yourself in every situation, and continual evolution. Every experience, be it good or bad, is an opportunity to progress. If you adopt this point of view, you no longer see failure as failure and success as success, but rather everything as an opportunity to learn something."

Are women better equipped to adopt agile leadership? I tend to think so. Alice Guilhon shared her experience that workplace atmosphere was always more consensual when women were in leadership roles or when there were a lot of women in the teams. There is more listening and less will to dominate a meeting. Women work for a project and not for their network. "At the Ministries of the Interior and the Defense, the importance of your network is perhaps more important that elsewhere. Men spend their time passing out their business cards. Building a network among men is part of their career development, while for women it is often more about opportunities and desire. Women have a goal and want to reach it. Men look to safeguard their perimeter and be heard." Her conclusion is not that management must be exclusively in the hands of women, but rather that you need to look for complementarity. "I believe a lot in balance. We have fought so hard for things not to be entirely masculine, if everything turns feminine, other problems will emerge. We need to be careful about that."

Barbara Belvisi agrees that men and women are completely different, and we need to cultivate this difference. Certain more feminine characteristics such as emotional sensitivity and humility stem from how girls are educated. As princesses are supposed to wait for a knight to rescue them, girls learn less about wielding a sword. As a result, a woman who knows 90 percent of what there is to know about a subject will tend to stay in the background, where a man who only knows 10 percent about a topic will go to front stage. In this respect, Barbara shared an original vision that deserves some contemplation. Should the only conclusion we draw from this unbalance be that we need to push women to try harder? "We are in a society that highly values showmanship and speaking out. You are a leader if you know how to communicate. Managers, those who get the promotions, are extroverts. We mistake charisma for competence. Isn't there room for another type of leadership? We need to make room for more women, but also for more people who have this sensibility. We need to rethink the leadership model for tomorrow. The ego needs to focus less on owning and more on contributing, even in large corporations."

Dare to be authentic

> If you are always trying to be normal, you will never know how amazing you can be.
> —Maya Angelou

People will follow you because you are different. Do not be afraid to have your own style. Dare to create something new and unexpected that stems from your authenticity, a personal style, and the continuous expression of your singularity. This does not necessarily mean great upheaval or radically innovative ideas. Above all, it is execution that will give this personal stamp.

Starting in 2007, I managed LeWeb from San Francisco, and the distance forced me to come up with an original management style. The idea of LeWeb arose from an inhabitual approach. We were two entrepreneurs in France and creating LeWeb was a way for us to develop a platform for entrepreneurs. We wanted to give them the means to achieve their ambitions by bringing together the entire ecosystem—investors, media, key Silicon Valley players—in a same place, in Paris, for a few days. To build this project, I began alone, from 2004 to 2006. My former husband managed the program content and I did the rest, including production, sponsors, and the attentive reception of all the guests in Paris. I was the project manager, the conductor, and somehow the hostess of the conference. But in 2006, we exceeded 1,000 participants, and I understood that I needed a team, and I needed it quickly. As I had probably matured a bit in my approach, I decided to trust men and women who were driven by the same desire to carry off a successful annual even. I didn't have employees, but used exclusively freelancers, independent artists or contractors, or people with their own businesses. I was organized down to the minute details. I composed the score and developed the framework, and everyone know their role and responsibilities. I left little room for improvisation in the process, in the sequence of steps, which didn't mean that I left no room for creativity. Quite to the contrary. I always thought it was important to build things together with others and that for everyone to flourish, everyone needed to contribute. I literally had ten different jobs every year. As the conference was held every year in December, we would meet at the beginning of March with five or six key people for a launch meeting, where we define the broad lines, the roadmap, the ideas, and what was going to be new. This was an opportunity to explore past errors so we didn't reproduce them. From that point on, everyone knew his or her role. At the same time, I never asked anyone to decide for me. I would listen, understand the context, and I was the one who took responsibility for the risks and the choices. It was fun that my teams affectionately called me "the boss."

Marion Carrette said something I find very true, "Online, you succeed by being yourself." Perhaps she and I were lucky in a way that is certainly less evident in other more standardized industries. My Little Paris, driven by Fany Pechiodat's original vision and personality, is one illustration. Fanny Bouton, who wears braids and has her first name in binary code tattooed on her neck, is another example of someone who has a personality all her own, who is radically authentic, and who has left her mark on French tech. She demonstrated how someone can take their own path with passion and difference, even in France, where we continue to believe that you necessarily need the "right" degree and all the expected labels to get anywhere. Fanny was born in 1972. Her father was a computer analyst and programmer and her mother was a nurse. Because of her father's profession, she grew up in code and quickly understood that computer science would keep evolving. After getting a Master's degree in art, she set out to be a drawing teacher but failed the secondary school teaching diploma examination three times. At the same time, having grown up with *Star Wars, Goldorak* and *Captain Future,* she loved robots and artificial intelligence. In 1997, at the beginning of the Internet bubble, the Gobelins Art School launched a training course with prerequisites in both coding and drawing. She got in and right afterwards she got a position as a webmaster in a company. She did this for six years, while following tech news and attending forums. She was one of the only women participating, and the men respected her for her technical expertise. More and more, she took on the role of moderator. At the age of 29, her career was stagnating, because her superior took away all her responsibilities when her two children were born.

To shake herself out of her boredom, Fanny organized a first in-real-life encounter of the people who participated in her favorite online forum, and that was how Fanny's Party was born. The next day, she got an email asking when the next event would be, and that pushed her to quit her job on a paid-training measure. She then took advantage of her unemployment benefits and aid for entrepreneurship to start her first company, Art-senic, and she founded the site fannysparty.com. Over the past 15 years, Fanny has organized a hundred or so Fanny's Parties, and these events have forged her place in the ecosystem. She began to be invited to press conferences, where she was the only high-tech blogger. When Typepad online blogging software came out in France, Nokia provided her with a phone which she used to post directly on her blog. In a few months, she reached 35,000 views a day, which was huge at the time. That was the beginning of online reputations and blogging. Every tech blogger ended up at her events, along with reporters, and it worked. The editor-in-chief of *Mobile Mag* contacted her, and paper magazines ask her to come work for them. In 2005-2006, she ended up on the Game One television channel, a mere twelve months after starting her company. So much for her former boss, who said she was throwing her career out the window.

In 2007, she hosted a live program with journalist and businessman Dominique Delport. She worked for a year at Direct 8, until her husband got transferred to Hong Kong and she had to follow him. There, she produced her first Web TV show called Tech Away. For two years, she met a lot of people and went frequently to Tokyo, while still organizing her events in Paris four times a year. When she got back to France, projects kept flowing in. In a chance meeting, the head of the HEC Business School digital course asked her to take over a class on digital communication for startups. So, she ended up working at a business school, when earlier a number of companies closed their doors to her because she didn't have a business school degree.

In her career, Fanny has done many different things, and held many day jobs, including cashier. She collected the refusal letters for internships, but as time went on, those that didn't want her as an intern were willing to pay her a lot as an extern. Being different can be a burden for a longtime, but it does mean you have to be clever and rebound all the time. Fanny likes the proverb, "If there is no solution, then there is no problem." Social media networks open incredible doors and can be a real pool of opportunities for those who leave the beaten path.

That said, large corporations offer more possibilities to be fully yourself than most people think. Today, Stéphanie Hospital is CEO and founder of the OneRagtime fund, but for a long time she worked in the corporate world, and that in no way kept her from being exactly who she intended to be, living in line with her *ikigai*. She finds her balance by spending a lot of time in the mountains and skiing a lot. "I always did exactly what I wanted to do. I prepared for business school, and when I didn't get into any in Paris, I decided to go to one in Grenoble because then I could ski. At the time, the school was not all that well ranked, but it was new and more innovative. It was just right for me, because the school was positioned in technology and innovation at a time when people weren't talking about these yet. I wanted to go into management and international marketing. I didn't have good grades, because I spent so much time skiing. When I graduated, I did auditing for Arthur Andersen for two years, and learned a lot, but I didn't like it at all. One of the partners was in charge of following an America's Cup challenge and I asked to be part of the project, which allowed me to move to consulting, which was better for me. I did that for three years, and then took a sabbatical to go boating. When I returned, I was hired by a client, Wanadoo (France Telecom), and I was finally able to do what I wanted, management and international product marketing. In 2000-2001, I turned to tech and innovation. I did that for 10 or so years at Wanadoo and then at the leading telecom operator Orange, where I grew. I've always been guided by what I wanted to do. The main threads have been international work, technological innovation, business development and management. I love building teams. I love people."

"When I was working at Orange," she continued, "the only thing that I asked was to be able to work Fridays from Chamonix, which is my favorite ski resort. My superior, Paul-François Fournier, was visionary when it came to work-life balance and shared my passion for the mountains. He accepted that I spend more time at Chamonix, and so I stayed. Since then, I have split my time between Paris and Chamonix, where my husband and my circle of friends are."

During her career at Orange, Stéphanie always had an intrepreneurial position. For three years, she found herself on the board of Dailymotion, an acquisition she had made at Orange and that was part of her responsibilities. Spending time every month with investors such as Philippe Colombel from Partech and Benoist Grossman from Idinvest got her interested in entrepreneurship. The idea matured in 2010 during a second sabbatical, spent skiing and traveling. She gives young women the following advice, "Dare to be who you are! If you want something, it is possible. When I started at Wanadoo, people told me that to rise in the ranks, I had to focus on the core business and not the 'little innovative stuff' I was doing. One of the top managers at Orange had also told that me, in 2002, but I don't follow along so easily. People also told me I didn't have enough of a sense of politics. Your strength is who you are, so it serves no purpose to go against your desires and what you want deep down. At the same time, you must continually focus on self-improvement and progress. In the telecom business in France between 2002 and 2010, there was a very typically French culture of 'it's got to be hard to be good.' I say that it's got to make me happy and be agreeable. Like with skiing, I'll give it my all for things that carry me away, but there has to be some notion of pleasure. I love excellence for the beauty of the gesture."

Being loyal to who you are also means defining your own criteria for success. For Amira Yahyaoui, being successful is first of all being personally proud of your accomplishments. It's also continuing to be able to look yourself in the mirror, even when you've made some hard decisions, such as firing someone or speaking harsh words, because you are convinced that what you have done was the right thing to do. Amira has strong values she puts directly into practice in her company, right down to operational details. When we interviewed her in 2018, she had just written her company's in-house rules. This charter includes some atypical clauses, but ones that are aligned with who Amira is and the ideas she defends. For example, her coworkers cannot expense meat-based meals. She also refuses to use leather chairs, for the same animal rights reasons. She forbids smokers from taking their breaks together. If they want to smoke, they have to go one by one. On the other hand, she will pay for absolutely everything that could help them stop smoking. These are not the usual things you find in such a business document, but Amira takes full responsibility for her conviction, and she doesn't force anyone to accept her conditions. I believe she is being very honest with her team. They know who they are working for. Taking responsibility for such personal and strong choices reveals a lot about your personality. Those who don't agree won't work in that company. It's a daring approach, but one that guarantees alignment.

We are quite far from the pseudo-authenticity that some business leaders stage on Instagram. Being authentic does not necessarily mean exposing your private life to the public eye to benefit your business. Maëlle Gavet has always clearly separated her private life and her professional life. Her public relations team recommended that she talk about her family on Instagram to appear more human, but for her the boundary was clear. "I have a problem with the implications for those around me. You do not have to expose your family and friends. I chose this career and the public aspects that go with it; they didn't. We can look perfectly human just by talking about our professional experience and the meetings we go to. We can also go beyond what is purely professional. I often talk about exhibitions that I will see, books I read, conferences, etc. For me, the rule is simple—my family is out of bounds. Everything else is acceptable, although frankly, I do not always understand why what I read should be public information. Compass has 1,000 employees and 3,000 agents, which makes enough people capable of seeing for themselves that I am not a robot. In the United States (and more and more elsewhere), there is a kind of cult of the personality. Leaders are like TV stars, they are expected to open their doors to the public and tell the story of their emotional lives. No one is obliged to accept this overexposure, which is for the most part a sham.

Authenticity has more to do with self-knowledge than with the ability to post selfies. Julie-Elya Hasson is very committed to personal development, which she has been practicing for decades. In particular, she spoke with us about the importance of identifying your limits and needs regarding work. "I co-founded or founded four companies with a three-year cycle in which the company operated but did not scale to several tens of millions of euros. I walked away from Stanford with three things: "Think big, iterate and kill the 'baby startup' (if not scalable)." When I'm in a large corporation, I know how to lead big teams and lead them to success. However, when I start from scratch, from a blank page, I give so much the first three years that I do not have enough spring to scale. So, if I have to start again, it will be either with one or several co-founders or through intra-entrepreneurship. The key is to transform your 'dysfunction' into a strength. It is better to have dysfunctions, they are in fact asperities that can identify where we excel. And from excellence and desire comes an alignment that makes it possible to succeed."

Be reliable

Earn trust, earn trust, earn trust. Then you can worry about the rest.

—Seth Godin

If you say you're going to do something, make sure you do it. This is the basis of your relationship with your teams, and it also opens the way for new opportunities. In companies, being reliable is very often a criterion of judgment. And that's the point I made about execution. Whatever happens, you have to get things done. One of my mottos is, "Under promise and over deliver."

In October 1995, my ex-husband was doing an assignment for Peugeot car manufacturer as part of a business school real life project. The idea was to launch an online car dealer. Given the context, it only took us a few weeks for me to quit my job, and we founded our first company, Looping Communications (very quickly renamed B2L, using the partners' initials—Bello Le Meur Lamotte—making a name much more in alignment with the world of communication agencies). We financed it with the 50,000 francs (the equivalent of $9000) that my paternal grandmother had given us at our wedding "to start life off well."

Our first customers trusted us, including Elida Fabergé, Peugeot, and others. We hired our first employees, and I experienced my first major entrepreneurial stress. As much as it is easy to make your own choices and sacrifices, it's not the same thing when other people depend on you at the end of the month. That's where I glimpsed the whole dimension of entrepreneurship—being an entrepreneur is like being skipper of a boat and on board are other people who trust you, and whom you do not have the right to betray. You can make mistakes, but you have to explain what happens transparently. And transparency is the most important thing to building and installing trust. You have to learn to move forward together, but you have a duty to be the leader of the troupe. A business leader is there to make the decisions.

For Rania Belkahia, anything is possible as long as you give yourself the means to achieve your ambition. At the beginning, carrying out a project requires a tremendous amount of energy invested in the concentration and focus, both of which must be found and maintained. "Focus is one of the most important things. When you're an entrepreneur and your business starts to take off, you're over-solicited, because there are not that many people on marketplace; you can quickly become a circus freak. At the beginning, it's important not to think about your self-interest. Being an entrepreneur is a social mandate. There are many ways to deviate from this mandate, through the abuse of corporate assets as well as by accepting invitations solely for personal interest, for example. Time is the rarest commodity. We must not act for personal interest, while we have the trust of our investors, customers and employees. Our focus is to create value. It's a social responsibility. You must put your company before yourself and not use it for personal communication."

The trust of others carries us and pushes us to surpass ourselves. It can mirror an image of our own value that we struggle to see alone. Frédérique Dame coaches many entrepreneurs, with whom she has developed a culture of trust. She can be tough with them, in a spirit of "spare the rod and spoil the child," like when you hit a tennis ball so that the other person sends it back harder. Working with these business leaders allows her to measure the breadth of what she learned during her years with Uber. "I see my true value when working with bright, entrepreneurial people and telling them things that make them better, that enlighten them, or when hearing conference organizers tell me the next day that the audience wants to implement my advice."

Chapter 5

You are not alone!

Your primary support system: your family

Whatever your goal is you will never succeed unless you let go of your fears and fly.

—Richard Branson

In 1995, when I co-founded my first business with my then-husband, I had very clearly chosen my career well before I graduated from business school. I am an only daughter. My mother raised me to be independent from a very young age. While being very protective and attentive, she made sure that I was not needy and that I could advance by myself.

At the age of 18, I left Perpignan, a small city its the south of France, with my partner and future husband to enter a preparatory class in Paris. I was lucky enough to grow up in a wealthy family, my father being a doctor and my mother a nurse, both throwing themselves into the unknown in 1970 when they settled in Perpignan, taking over the practice of a retiring doctor.

I grew up pampered. My parents always took me when they traveled to Africa (where my maternal grandparents were based and my mom grew up) and to the United States (where my father, as an ENT surgeon, went for conventions so he could stay at the forefront of field). I was lucky. I grew up in a small provincial town and had an opening to the world. I also grew up inspired by strong women, starting with my mother, in a very matriarchal culture. I did not have to look very far for my role models. They were around me, in my family, and they were also there to support me in my choices.

I have Corsican roots on my mother's side. My great-grandmother had five children and ran a hosiery shop. She was one of the first women to have her driver's license and car. At the time, she was considered a person who did not fit in the box, "a woman of ill repute" as she said herself. On my father's side, my grandmother was French and born in Algeria, a war widow, who quickly shared her motto with me—"What hand will you get out of this situation? It's the one you have on your arm" (she did not say it in such a polite way). She completed her self-taught career as a psychiatric hospital director, a male realm at the time. I think my mother's image also influenced me a lot. My parent's entrepreneurial adventure was that of running a medical practice in a small provincial town. My father was the doctor, and he did nothing else. My mother did the rest. She orchestrated their professional life as a COO would in a perfectly tuned duo, never leaving room for her doubts, always animated by a fierce constructive energy.

The family is our first influence. Similarly, it can also be our first support system. Maïa Baudelaire's passion for nutrition comes from her mother and her grandfather, who lived to be a hundred thanks to an extraordinary lifestyle. Delphine Bellini's concern for her team comes directly from her entrepreneur father. Marion Carrette was also lucky to have both father and grandfather entrepreneurs. It was her father who lent her the money to start out. When she created her first company, ECRITO, she called her father for advice in the early days. When she later did not need him, she missed the bond with him. Marion's mother devoted herself to raising her children. In a way, Marion chose a life that combined that of her two parents. Clémentine Piazza found her first models in her family, too. "I have two brothers and a feminist father and mother. I believe that the family plays a crucial role in the development of a girl's ability to overcome the obstacles that are unfortunately still present in our society. Your close circle should wish success upon you. It is essential to be surrounded by people who want your freedom and who prefer you when you are strong." Marion Moreau's father was also the first to encourage her to take risks. He reassured her that she could do a different job from the others (Marion has a brother and a sister who are artists).

Mathilde Thomas's best mentors were also her parents. Her father, a down-to-earth man from the mountains, took over the family business and founded the sporting chain Go Sport. When Mathilde and her husband founded Caudalie, they called him every three days to ask him questions. Mathilde's mother ran a communications agency that she sold to McCann, which proved to be a great help for communication, branding and advertising. After five years, the students exceeded their teachers, who knew nothing about cosmetics.

Your mentors

> *I've learned that people will forget what you said, people will forget what you did, but people will never forget how you made them feel.*
>
> —Maya Angelou

Today, it is easy to find people to share your experience. Do not hesitate to rely on your community. From childhood, we have been told that it is better to be strong, so that you are not seen to be a victim. On the contrary, I think that sensitivity can be a strength, but that we must know how to channel it. Try to open up to share experiences, doubts, fears, and hesitations with people you trust, or people simply going through the same steps (I see the strength of the group effect among startups in The Refiners). The days of entrepreneurs who did not want to share their ideas are over. Everyone understands that the more you enrich your idea by opening it to outside contributions, the more you have the opportunity to build it solidly. You will be surprised at the support you will receive. There are some rules to follow—be optimistic, ban preconceived ideas, refuse to fit into a mold, and surround yourself with people who are different from you, who inspire you and teach you new things. But beyond that, you have to be honest with yourself and know what drives you, why you get up to in the morning. This is how you will be most likely to get frank feedback from your mentors and your teams.

In her career as a business creator, Fleur Pellerin regrets not having been able to discuss with other entrepreneurs about topics such as the partners' pact. These very technical aspects are not necessarily obvious, and the experience of others in this area can be very useful. "Starting a business is a very lonely experience," says Fleur. "I realize how very valuable the accumulated experience of others is. In the heat of the moment, we do not necessarily think about asking for help, and we do not necessarily have people we trust. It's probably something I missed. If I were to go through the initial construction phase again, I would seek help or advice from people who had done it before." When you set up a business, try to find answers, do not stay alone with your problems, even on very basic aspects.

Mentoring is essential. Just as there are agents and coaches for top athletes, it is important for entrepreneurs to have mentors to rely on. It is valuable to be able to share your fears, doubts and dreams, and to be able to share in confidence. It is also valuable to know how to listen, and to do the same for others.

At The Refiners, we offer startups highly operational mentorship. A fun fact about the difference in mentalities between France and the United States: I am often asked in France how I compensate mentors of the program. A coach is paid, but a mentor is a volunteer by definition. This is precisely what gives him or her extraordinary freedom. Of course, you can find an "official" mentor through a mentoring program or a network of entrepreneurs. It was a mentor from the Entreprendre network who encouraged Fany Pechiodat to raise her ambitions, saying: "I won't mentor you if you do not add a zero to your goal." It helped a lot. But often you find your best support in a rather informal way, by enjoying the meetings.

"I had a lot of dads and moms," says Amira Yahyaoui. "I was lucky enough to have access to some very exceptional people, who really treated me kindly. They opened doors I never would have been able to open. Someone had done it for them and they paid it forward. I hope I will do the same myself." Opening doors is not necessarily easy. For example, it is always the same people who are invited to participate in round tables, and when we recommend another lesser-known person who deserves some of the limelight, she or he is not necessarily accepted. Yet, as Amira rightly points out, all known people began by not being known. At some point, someone was bold enough to push them to the forefront. Among her mentors, she has many more men than women.

For a long time, she thought it was because women did not give back enough, but in fact, since the majority of people who rise above the others are men, it is mathematical that we find more men to pull us up.

As the founder of a political NGO, Amira had the opportunity to participate in many conferences. The Davos conference in particular gave her access to powerful people, some of whom were of great help to her. Amira is also very grateful to Garrett Camp and the risks taken by Expa to help her in her entrepreneurial project.

Alice Guilhon, the Dean of SKEMA, benefited a lot from being mentored by older men throughout her life. When she was a child, her tennis coach taught her tenacity. When she left the university, she got support from a faculty member. When she worked at the Ministry of the Interior and Defense, her husband, a policeman, protected her in an environment where she was at great risk as she was one of the few women, and the youngest. All of them gave their help not expecting anything in return, but no doubt thinking that since Alice worked more than the others, she would certainly be very effective.

Frédérique Dame also had practically only male mentors. She can depend on a powerful community of trusted men who are there for her, and who make her aware of aspects of herself that she would never have seen (starting with her own qualities). Every year, she does a comprehensive overview of her situation with one of them. If she has a question, they answer her right away. She also has a circle of friends that inspires her and that she inspires with her successes and the challenges she has overcome. "Having friends who share similar experiences is comforting and allows you to move forward with greater confidence. If she did it, I can do it too." Mentoring is a give-and-take system, and those who have been lucky enough to be mentored inevitably want to be supportive in turn. "I like to help, to inspire people so that they push their limits, and to help them take their raw material and make gold."

The way you find yourself a mentor is not, as we all too often think, to look for someone and ask them if they want to be a mentor. It should develop from a relationship. For Maëlle Gavet, there is no overall mentor, but different mentors for different moments and subjects. Her advice is to identify a network of people who can be consulted on specific topics. "Women do not spend a lot of time building an informal network because they are too busy taking care of their families. As a result, they often do not have this pool of mentors to whom they can ask questions. I have a list of people around the world that I can question. Last week, I was wondering how to change the culture of a company that doubles in size every six months, and I went to see two people. However, I will not go see them every month. Do not send me an email asking, "Do you want to be my mentor?" Instead you could say, "I need to negotiate my salary and I do not know how to do it," and it would be a pleasure for me to answer your question. This kind of network works through mutual trust. I have benefited so much and continue to benefit from people who have spent 15 minutes (or more) with me, free of charge, and to whom I feel indebted. The problem is that people often contact me without substance. I have a packed timetable, so if I'm about to dedicate half an hour to someone, I must know what the problem I will help solve is.

This notion of efficiency and respect for the other's time is essential. Corinne Vigreux, the founder of TomTom, does not have a lot of available time, but she always helps women in need. Some come to see her every quarter with a list of questions. In general, the people she mentors are very organized and respectful of the time that Corinne dedicates to them. They send her questions by email in advance so that she can prepare her answers. "Allowing an entrepreneur to avoid making mistakes is very satisfying," says Corinne. "I met a young woman during a pitch she had won, who wanted to give 30 percent of her company for not much. I told her, 'Do not do that, dilute as little as possible.' Four years later, she's at 4 million in sales. She did not dilute it at all. She's on track and calls me when she has a need, always for specific questions.

Rachel Delacour works the same way. She did not have only one mentor, but benefited from the help of a lot of people who gave her ten minutes of their time to enlighten her on very specific topics. The key is to put yourself in the shoes of the person you want to question, starting with being curious about her (Rachel spent a lot of time peeling through LinkedIn profiles, for example).

Do not hesitate to use the services of a professional, a coach or even a psychologist when you feel that you do not have the right strategy. When Clémentine Piazza was Marketing Director of Unibail Rodamco, her team had 150 people. As a result, very early she thought about the kind of leader she wanted to become. "I was faced with old real estate wolves, in a male world. I needed to gain confidence and define my way of federating people around my projects. I had to move very quickly. My challenge was to know myself. I worked on my personal development, thanks to the fabulous tools that exist today, and through Unibail, I got a professional coach that allowed me to advance quickly. Coaching is a science and provides very valuable support to clearly find the right place as soon as possible is. When you are in your place, flow settles in very naturally. Otherwise, you dry up." Clémentine has also been very inspired by models like Stephanie Cardot, another entrepreneur who founded To Do Today, who is very committed and whose experience and fighting spirit helped her.

Odile Roujol thought she could have taken more time to meet people throughout her career. The meetings continue through conversations, feeding us and helping us grow, and allowing us to release the pressure. "A more relaxed Odile would not necessarily have been less successful, would have experienced a better daily life, and it would have been better for my teams, too," she says. "I encourage all the entrepreneurs I know to have mentors, advisors, and then independent board members. This is the best way to continue to grow. It took me too long, despite my success, to realize that these encounters help to get some distance, to put things in perspective, and ultimately save us a lot of time, making us more successful. I understood this by being on a board of directors, which did not prevent me from doing a very good job at Orange."

Investors and employees of a company can also be mentors in their own way. Céline Lazorthes's mentors are Catherine Barba, a successful French tech entrepreneur who spent five years on her board of directors, and Xavier Niel, who was one of its shareholders. "Xavier is very caring, appreciative and encouraging. He told me: 'Never let yourself be told that you have a small business!'"

Marion Carrette was inspired by the pragmatism and impetus that Loïc brought to her when she worked with us at B2L, but also by tech pioneer and entrepreneur Marc Simoncini in his role as investor. "Marc brought solutions. We struggled for two years to find a car insurance willing to partner with us. Marc is the one who unblocked the situation by coming with me to the meeting with the insurance company. These are two people I admire. Both trusted me eyes closed. When you get that kind of trust you need to merit it." Thanks to this trust game, customers too can be inspiring and exemplary. The customers that Sibylle de Villeneuve chooses all have something that will inspire her to be better. Today, she is also part of the Women Initiative Foundation mentoring program, which gave her ways to gain confidence, be more assured of her choices, and support what she claimed.

The role of mentor can quickly become a form of sponsorship. Delphine Bellini is a member of the Institut Français de la Mode Executive MBA Business Creation Jury, and is often very impressed by the quality of the projects presented. She points out that when you become a mentor to an entrepreneur, it is because you believe in the person's project and their ability to carry it out. This conviction very often leads to becoming the project's "ambassador" as well as that of the person who leads it.

Helen Bouygues, on the other hand, makes a clear difference between the mentor, who will provide advice, and the sponsor, who will allow an individual to accelerate her career within a company. Both are important. In her very masculine work environment, Helen lacked inspiring role models. She has had many mentors who have objectively helped accelerate her career, but she notes that in four out of five cases, the relationship was ambiguous in their head (never during work, but often after). In her experience, it is often difficult for women to find sponsors, especially in a male environment, where men do not necessarily have the habit of working with women and are not completely comfortable with it. In companies like Merrill Lynch, men support each other through networks such as the Princeton football team alumni club. Companies need to find mechanisms to make it more natural for women to find sponsors. We can also find mentors who are not in the same professional environment. A coach or a husband could be a mentor.

Julie-Elya Hasson has not had a mentor in the traditional meaning of the term but, depending on the period of her life and the subject matter, she has had people who served as coaches and inspiration. An influential woman human resources manager, whose career unfolded in the CAC40 corporation, helped her advance her career. She also draws inspiration from other entrepreneurs who are among her friends— Fany Pechiodat, founder of My Little Paris, for perfect execution; Françoise Mercadal-Delassale, president of the French bank Crédit du Nord, for her capacity to lead on a large scale, to be bold and innovate; and Fanny Picard, founder of the AlterEquity fund, because she is visionary and for her ethics. However, having a mentor in the traditional sense does not match her personality. Fortunately, we can work things out perfectly without mentor. She is the proof of that, and so am I. It is essential to surround yourself with the right people and listen to suggestions, being inspired by others all the time.

Depending on your temperament, you can share your progress in a group or do a personal assessment every month. The key is to set up milestones to reassure yourself, to have points of reference when you are feeling unsure of things. In my case, when I'm feeling stressed, I have a very personal and lonely side that expresses itself. I need to hit rock bottom before to giving a kick to rise to the surface again; this allows me to take stock of the degree and reasons for my stress. I often see situations all the way through, and then I take them head-on. With the exception of The Refiners, I founded all my businesses with someone else. Even though I did not always share my stress, I did not experience the entrepreneurial adventure alone.

Your circle

> *Keep away from people who try to belittle your ambitions. Small people always do that, but the really great make you feel that you, too, can become great.*
> —Mark Twain

Knowing yourself well is the prerequisite for any adventure. It is also the starting point for building strong and complementary teams around you. "Being aware of who you are, what you love, and what inspires you is important. You can then surround yourself with people who give you positive energy, but who are also better than you at certain skills," says Odile Roujol. "A strong team means being a conductor and playing with different scores and registers. If everyone has the same profile and the same culture, it is comfortable, but it is a model that is much less creative, less innovative and ultimately less powerful."

For Fany Pechiodat, in order to run the entrepreneurial marathon, it is important to know what gives you energy and what takes it away. Like a smartphone, each of us has a limited amount of energy. "Answering an email on a legal issue drains my energy, while doing something creative energizes me. The first years, I slept two hours a night, and I was not at all tired. You have to surround yourself with people based on this problem of energy, otherwise you run the risk of getting tired too quickly. If we give a lot, but we receive a lot, we hold on." At the time of our interview, in October 2017, her six original partners were always at her side, strong in their complementarity. Everyone encountered dips in the road, but none at the same time. Bruno, one of her associates, told her one day, "We will make a deal, I take all the negative energy, you take all the positive energy." Nothing is more valuable than being supported by a team.

In 2016, the Paris Pionnières team (now Willa) was reduced to two people, and Caroline Ramade had to do almost everything. Based on the principle that you do things poorly when you have to force yourself, she defined her needs so that the association could function at its best, starting by assessing what she was good at and how useful it was. Her levers are creativity, strategy, and vision, and she is also good at bringing in money and attracting project ambassadors. On the other hand, she is not in her comfort zone when it comes to managing everyday operations. So, she designed her team to fill in the areas she was lacking. She found someone to follow operations in her absence, an ecosystem specialist for communication and monitoring, and someone to manage the space, which took 40 percent of her time. She was able to free up a lot of mental space.

Before Céline Lazorthes passed the Leetchi.com torch to Alix Poulet, she still held most of the hiring interviews and accompanied all the managers in implementing annual interviews. She chose not to have an HR manager because she considers that the utmost attention should be paid to hiring, and that entrusting this mission to a non-specialist in human resources gives that person a lot of responsibility. Each of Leetchi's managers is responsible for the people they hire. The selection is hard during the trial period, but in the end the company has almost no turnover once people are on the job. Employees recruited at the beginning of the venture are still there, and all the managers have been there since the beginning. Céline advises entrepreneurs to surround themselves with positive people. "Since I did not have a co-founder at the start, I surrounded myself with people who wanted to experience the entrepreneurial adventure. I have never lacked trust in my managers. We are all in the same boat, and I have never felt alone. All my managers are people I am very close to, even though I would not say they are friends. It takes a relationship of trust."

Alix Poulet, who succeeded Céline at the head of Leetchi, is a women entrepreneur who sold her first business. Teams at Leetchi accepted her easily, finding her particularly attentive, caring, and human, but also very professional and involved. Celine instilled her personality and values in the company, hiring employees who had the same mindset and then went on to hire people like themselves. She echoed the words of the founder of the online real-estate site MeilleurAgents, who told her that the greatest pride moment of pride what to have a "business without assholes." Skills evolve, but behavior does not change, so she was most attentive to the latter, focusing on values of caring, mutual help, listening, and learning from each other. Laure, the CTO, did not know the dot.net when she joined the company, but that was not the most important. Over time, the management team has grown, and she has developed more skills.

"There is a balance to be found, as we face issues that are very burdensome, and a world where there is no room for error. I am lucky to have people around me who have the same attachment to the company as I do. I think our CTO would have left for a bigger salary if she had been a man. Since, she has largely recovered the fruit of her labor with her shares. I would do anything to fight for my coworkers. I have a strong need for justice."

Her coworkers are a great source of inspiration for her. "I am convinced that we are innovating because we have gathered a lot of different profiles. We have a lot of foreign coworkers, a bit by chance and perhaps because we were looking for people with a very adaptable character and expatriates are accustomed to the gymnastics of adaptation. There are people with incredible career paths. Adil, our caretaker, is passionate about developing websites, so Leetchi is funding his training to be a web developer. This kind of beautiful triangle helps companies retains their employees and becomes a very virtuous pact if it touches everyone. Once a month, from 9:30 to 10 a.m., we have a breakfast where we present the projects. Adil is there every time." This diversity and the trust employees have provide Céline with great motivation as a business leader.

Delphine Bellini is used to telling new entrepreneurs that their greatest strength lies in those who surround them, be it their teams, their suppliers or their customers. "Your network and your circle are your strength. My entire career has been conditioned by the encounters and human adventures that form the foundation of a project and its success. We do not do anything alone."

When she left the management of the JC de Castelbajac fashion house, Delphine had the opportunity to start a consulting business advising and supporting high-end and luxury designer brands, and thus to touch on different dimensions of a wide range of issues concerning strategic orientation, brand identity, organizational structure, financial management, and international deployment, among others. She was not aware of the power and importance of this network. "Things happened by themselves, or almost. It was under the impulse of Didier Grumbach, who was then president of the Haute Couture federation, that I started to support creators on specific assignments of varying lengths. Then, during my meetings, other assignments arrived. I was not at all aware of it. I was not even on LinkedIn. Then I realized that to carry out my assignments, I was calling on a lot of people from different sectors (suppliers, service providers, manufacturers, lawyers, financiers, etc.) that I knew, making the contact and getting them involved in the projects. I made connections. It was easy, efficient and beneficial to all stakeholders. It is also through consulting that I ended up at Schiaparelli. All this is part of you, you do not calculate; it is built from meeting to meeting."

Women do not necessarily have the reflex to deliberately build their network. Too often they see meetings as a waste of time, when they are the basis of creating relationships over the long term. For Alice Guilhon, lack of boldness is also why women are reluctant to rely on existing networks—they are not sure of their place. Stéphanie Hospital was very impressed by the advice given to her by the head hunter Ahmad Hassan, whom she met when she was 28 or 29 years old. "You have a very good career, but your network is exclusively inside Orange. You have to open up, meet people outside, and build a network." This is a recommendation that she has applied for years.

Your business partners

We rise by lifting others.
—Robert Ingersoll

Together, we are stronger, and we go further. "When you're young and you do not know much, it's better to be two," said Mathilde Thomas, the founder of Caudalie. But I think it's just as important when you're not so young and you are more experienced. According to Julie-Elya Hasson, it is particularly important for a woman to start a business with one or more partners, because the fundamental nature of the woman's strength is to question, which can sometimes lead to doubts. It is a strength to question yourself, and it is necessary to have reassurance. It is key to know the person you are partnering with, and to make the partnership last over time. Julie had the experience of starting a company and being joined by a woman she had known for a few years, but the transition did not work out because her partner was from a large corporation and was used to having things move forward on their own between two meetings. This does not happen in a startup. You have to own all the issues and be on deck keeping ideas alive and turning them into reality. So you have to make sure that your associates have real entrepreneurial spirit and put their energy in everything, from the details to the comprehensive whole. This is especially at the beginning. You have to get your hands dirty. In my opinion, the idea is secondary to the execution. And the people are very important. In the startups I select for The Refiners, I am particularly attentive to the founding team. With a partner, there is already a corporate culture, and values that infuse into the business. I often say that "fish always rot from the head down." A disagreement between partners will inevitably have deleterious repercussions for the project.

The difficulty is that from the outset you do not necessarily perceive the true nature of the people in front of you. This is what Isabelle Bordry experienced. "The trap that I discovered along the way is that when you want to partner, there is an initial dynamic that is very positive around an idea, and driven by this impetus, you can let down your guard more than you would when hiring someone. We rarely interview our future partners. And when we do find ourselves at the same desk facing difficulties, we become aware of differences and often it's too late."

Partnerships should refuse all competition. It is imperative to establish the rules from the start. My youngest son, Grégoire, rows on the under-19 American junior team, and I think this sport is a good illustration. At first glance, the sport does not seem very technical. You imagine that the rowers' synchronization and strength are what count. Nothing could be farther from reality. In a boat of eight, the place and the role of each person is very important and must be accepted by everyone so that the boat moves forward best. The role of the helmsman is to direct the boat, to decide the tactics to adopt, to establish and maintain the speed and pace of the strokes. The first rower behind him is the one who gives the impulse and the tempo. The five rowers in the middle are usually the strongest and send in the power, while the last two stabilize the boat. These nine "partners" are not in competition with each other but are all rowing in the same direction with a common goal and a mission to accomplish. It's not enough to have the eight strongest rowers to have the best boat.

Even when the partnership is not between a couple, it is still necessary to consider the situation of divorce and not delude yourself. Anticipating this possibility does not mean provoking it. A good way to guard against unpleasant surprises is to set up a vesting clause between the founders. The time required for the implementation of all of the company's actions, as originally agreed, conditions the shares. Thus, if one of the founders decides to leave after a year, he will only be entitled to the agreed part corresponding to his involvement for one year.

"I think it's very important to have a balance between men and women among the partners," says Marion Carrette. "When there are only men, competition is quick to rise, and it is rebalanced as soon as there are women." Throughout my career, I have only been associated with men, and I have found it very interesting.

When Loïc and I divorced, we also stopped working together. At that time, I took stock of all my strengths. What had I capitalized on? What did I want to learn? What were promising fields? I did not go find new partners. LeWeb, for me, was not a conference company, but a connection between people. The idea I had about what followed came down to this question: How can we continue to help entrepreneurs? I met Carlos during a pitch contest organized for high school students at the French school of San Francisco. He had plans to set up an accelerator with Pierre, an entrepreneur friend with whom he played music. He suggested I invest. I stopped him right away and said, "I'm not interested in investing. On the other hand, it is so aligned with the reflection that I am leading today that it would interest me to do it together with you." In 48 hours, we decided to embark on the adventure together. Our partnership formed through serendipity.

You have to decide your place from the beginning. What you can bring to the building? Carlos works very well with startups on creativity. Pierre is very didactic. I am more of a catalyst for communication and the network. With partners, regardless of whether they are men or women, you have to define each person's place and ensure that there is no overlap. It is less a question of "defining the roles" than it is delineating the fields of action. It also means accepting trust. There are things you do not touch, decisions that are made unilaterally. Otherwise there would be no complementarity and I would not see the interest of being three.

The most difficult to manage in a partnership is the inevitable part of affect and ego. How to avoid entering into competition? Note that three is not the best number for a partnership, because we naturally tend to do two plus one, with triptychs that reconfigure. The most natural is the pair. What matters to me for The Refiners is to be able to tell myself that in the end, we will have done something good and accomplished our mission, especially as we embarked investors along for the ride. They entrusted us with their funds and we have nearly 60 startups.

Complementarity is very important. This is typically the strength of the pair formed by Afrimarket's founding team. Rania Belkahia met her partner Jérémy during her end-of-studies internship at Télécom Paris in a subsidiary of the Bolloré group. Jérémy was Africa Director there, with ten years of experience on the African continent, while Rania had only done internships (including one at Elior, whose president is one of their investors today). The two colleagues began to discuss a few business ideas and, once Rania started her masters in entrepreneurship, they decided to launch the company. Rania really appreciates this twosome inspired by the same common goal. For her, diversity in education and culture is a true added value. She sees the partnership (like all other relationships) to be an everyday investment, work in and of itself, that you need to nourish and take care of.

Complementary skills in the founding team may have played a major role in the longevity of TomTom and the fact that it has been able to pivot effectively several times. One had a financial vision, two engineers carried the technical part, and Corinne Vigreux did all the rest, namely sales, marketing, and operations. "In times of growth, we were really united as a management team. We had a great deal of confidence in the topics we are competent in. It allowed us to go deeply into the important things, and we managed to multiply our efforts." The particularity of this team was that Corinne's husband was among them, which could have played a role in cohesion. "We were never in conflict over the strategy and the risks, nor were we in conflict as a couple. We gave everything we had to the company several times over. It could have gone bad too." What guided them in their choices was a shared vision. In the beginning, they made products for the general public for personal digital assistant, that by their ease of use and their performance, widely democratized navigation. Acquiring their mapping tool and technological innovations provided real-time traffic information, which helped reduce congestion and offer better route planning. Today, TomTom is embarking on the great adventure of autonomous driving. This shared vision is based on the different qualities of each one, each knowing exactly what he or she must do. "This collective intelligence is probably also a key to success. There is always one to lift the morale of the others. We manage to support each other, and there is a group dynamic that works well. Beyond the professional context, we have formed a strong bond of friendship. We have shared such powerful moments, like the IPO. The after is not the same as the before."

Entrepreneurial couples

> *Coming together is a beginning, staying together is progress, and working together is success.*
> —Henry Ford

There is nothing more difficult than a business partnership. People often say, "I could never work with my spouse." Yet, in a couple, there are deep strengths that can bolster working together. With my ex-husband, we each had our own playground. We never decided how to divide the roles we would play in our businesses. This occurred naturally based on our respective affinities. At the time, I do not think it was a question of actually splitting the skills needed, but simply of identifying in which fields one or the other would be most effective at a moment's notice. For example, in the 2000s, when we launched Ublog (which became Typepad/Six Apart France), a whole territory had to be cleared. Blogs (or publishing content that a community can react to without any technical knowledge) were in their infancy. There was a lot of evangelistic work to do on the market, and it involved a lot of meetings, especially in the evening, and a lot of content production. Loïc naturally took on this role. With three children aged 8, 6 and 2 at home, I was not willing to go to meetups that were often organized informally around communities of Internet users in Parisian bars. This was when Fanny Bouton launched Fanny's Party, which met with great success (see page 88). I stayed behind the scenes watching over the less visible part of managing the company, in partnership with Olivier Creiche, who was already at our side at the time of B2L, our first company. To enjoy my life as a mother, I chose not to go out, but I did provide technical support by answering requests from my home, often between 8:30 p.m. and 11 p.m. while waiting for my ex-husband to come back. I created a lot of activity with multiple email addresses. When your team is small, you become creative, hiding behind "contact," "support," and "info" email addresses. I even invented names. Few people actually knew that I was the one answering, and that led to some funny situations.

Our collaboration was deep and complementary and worked extremely well from a business point of view. We met at the age of 16, married at 20, and started to work together from scratch. The work was part of what held us together, and we never had a problem talking about it at night or at breakfast. I remember one morning, a few weeks before one of the last editions of LeWeb. We were at home, having coffee, when all of a sudden I said, "It's Black Friday, we need to take advantage of it." We launched a Black Friday sale at 7:30 a.m. and sold 150 tickets in an hour.

The other crucial element for us was complete trust in one another. We had always made key decisions together. Communication is central to reaching a consensus and to staying afloat during tough times.

It was easy with Loïc because I didn't reason from a place of ego, but from a place of family, which is very different. We were never wrestling or racing each other. I had my family, and it was my family that succeeded. Sometimes, I realized that if I left my framework, he had a hard time accepting it; over time, confidence dissipates. In 2006, I decided to put myself more in the forefront. You must not let others convince you that you don't know how to do certain things. Do not compete, choose balance, but impose yourself. A couple is like an ocean. At times, the sea is blue; at others, there are storms. You have to know how to reef at the right time.

When I met Isabelle Bordry, she was not yet an entrepreneur. She used to watch Loïc and me with astonishment, because it did not make sense to her to work as a couple. But the paths of entrepreneurship are impenetrable, and nearly 20 years later she co-founded Retency with her partner Xavier. At the root of their venture was a taste for freedom and a passion for American and digital culture she had discovered at Yahoo! They loved the startup mode made of speed, action with measurable impact, clearing new ground, agility, and breaking patterns. "How can we create value differently?" This question stayed with her. Three years ago, she and her husband began to wonder about the best way to help traditional players work with the same tools as those in the digital world. In the latter, we can get a lot of information about customer behavior, which helps to clarify the types of services that we develop. In the physical world, it's much more difficult to know what's going on between the front door and the checkout line. Isabelle's husband, Xavier, was a banker and a trained engineer. At 40, he wanted to return to his first love. He quickly became interested in connected objects, for the ubiquity they confer, and built a first platform to test temperature (used for refrigerators at Paris's central wholesale food market, among other places). One day, Isabelle read an article explaining how Amazon uses data to improve customer service and cross-sell. The idea took root and, from one point to another, the couple created a device to allow brands to collect information via smartphone to understand the impact of their advertising actions. The team led by Xavier set up an algorithm that provides indicators about the visitor journey equivalent to those that can be obtained on the Internet, in full respect of consumer digital privacy.

When we spoke with Isabelle, they were in full deployment. "When we decided to start, we were both at a time in our lives where we said to ourselves 'Why not?' At first, I said 'I'll help Xavier—he is the president. This is working well, because our personalities are very complementary, we complete each other professionally. There have been surreal moments when he asked me with whom I went to lunch. It was odd. It has been complicated to stop discussing work when we cross the threshold at home. We are managing to do it now, but there was a moment when it was a burden, because work was our only topic of discussion. I have experienced difficult partnerships before, and I find this easier."

Complementarity is also at the heart of Rachel Delacour's beautiful entrepreneurial story with her husband, Nicolas. After graduating from business school and working her first job at Carrefour, at the age of 25, Rachel was poached by Bata to develop the brand's management control system in France. When she arrived at Bata, she did not have the software she needed to analyze data from different databases to understand the cost structure and find possible optimizations. She was frustrated in her day-to-day work, not having enough budget or any reporting tools worthy of the name. She did not get support from the internal IT teams, who were male in their fifties and a hundred miles away from understanding what she was trying to do. She found the support she was looking for in the company in her partner. He was an engineer in business analytics and began to help her write specifications for a tool that fit her budget. Gradually, they came to the same conclusion—existing tools were too complex and inaccessible. There is a gap to fill on a huge global market. This was 2008, and Amazon was starting to show that it was possible to develop BtoB software as a service (SAAS) tools and companies like Salesforce were creating business models that were holding their own. Driven by a strong conviction, they decided to go into cloud business intelligence.

When they started, Rachel and Nicolas did not have much to lose. They brought a very new perspective that allowed them to be disruptive. They left their respective jobs and moved in with Nicolas's mother in the South of France. They did not know at that time that they were creating a startup, because there was as much information about it as there is now. Completely outside the circuit, not knowing that they could interest incubators, they spent a year coding. With only 15,000 euros in savings to launch their project, there was a great sense of urgency. While Nicolas provided the technical part, Rachel spent her time on LinkedIn talking about their idea and building an important base of user feedback and prospects. This first year allowed them to understand that their market was primarily abroad, and certainly not in France. They found IT managers much more receptive to the idea in the United States. Having no desire to go overseas, they worked with web conferencing, SAAS and distance selling, and building an online community. Incubators began to notice them, but their mode of operation was to carefully execute rather than make noise. They filled out only one application, for a competition from the Ministry of Research, which got them a grant so they could hire their first trainee engineers. They immediately moved on to raising funding to go further faster. Relying on their personal network, they brought in American business angels who contributed what Rachel calls "American-style kicks in the butt," bringing with them a culture of software, sales, lead generation, and KPIs.

Rachel and Nicolas's vision was to put business intelligence in everyone's hands. "We only did that, and we did it with passion. It's also because we did it as a couple, so we thought about what we were doing 24 hours a day. We were both in the same boat, and I think it brought us both a lot. One of us was always there to support the other. I have a lot more compassion for spouses of entrepreneurs who are not in the boat, than for the couples who start a business together. As a couple, you do not work twice as much, but four times more. Our communication was so smooth, that it allowed us to avoid all the psychodrama that can occur with co-founders. Venture capitalists immediately understood how complementary we were as a couple and how that multiplied the strengths of the project."

"We wanted our project to conquer the world," continues Rachel. "We had global ambitions from the first day. And at the same time, we did not consider our company as our baby. We did not want to protect it, but to open the floodgates. This entity that was being built could also be killed by competition from Silicon Valley. We thought that since it might be shot down from one moment to the next anyway, we could not afford to set aside our private life. When we started talking about having kids, it was pretty natural. Our first was born in 2010. It was financially difficult, but we wanted to make room for to our personal lives. We had the same vision. The first year was complicated for us as a couple because you judge yourself professionally, and it's hard to hear that from your other half. But that's normal because at the beginning, the roles are so intertwined that you have to have an opinion on everything. We tried to see beyond that. I always call Nicolas 'my co-founder.' We did not hide the fact that we were married, but we did not put it in the forefront either, so as not to look too much like a traditional family business, with the man doing the baking and the woman selling the bread. This is also why we do not have the same last name, not to mention that I had an interest in keeping my maiden name because of natural referencing on the Internet.

"What I really like as a couple is that there is always one to catch the other," she says. "Sometimes we both had low morale, and in the end, with a good night's sleep, we'd be off and running again. It's wonderful to share the moments of euphoria related to a fundraiser or an important signature. This strengthens and spices up any couple's life, giving it a lot more depth."

If you do start a business as a couple, I really invite you to pay close attention to the structure of the governance and to provide a fair and protective framework for everyone. The most difficult part is not during, but when you stop or sell your company, it's completely different and you may, unfortunately, start taking different paths. When we had lunch with Barbara Belvisi in December 2017, she had made the still unofficial decision to leave the board of directors of the Hardware Club. Barbara had partnered with her mate and a friend, putting all her eggs in one basket—her passion, her life as a couple, and the company. When disagreements between founders mingled with her personal life, everything became more complicated. Barbara decided to leave in a very professional and elegant way, rather than embarking on a power struggle between partners. In retrospect, she thought she should have structured the governance differently by having another female present on the board.

Chapter 6
Opening possibilities for women

For the emergence of a new sisterhood

The success of every woman should be the inspiration to another. We should raise each other up.

—Serena Williams

When Alice Guilhon took over the reins of SKEMA Business School, she was not yet 40 years old. "We had a plenary meeting with the entire team and a woman said, 'In any case, we'll have to keep a close eye on Alice, because she's a woman, she's young, and we don't know if she'll succeed.' Three months later, she congratulated me." Older men often protected Alice, and more often than not, women were the ones who would throw a monkey wrench into the works. Because of their insecurities, women could still tend to slow down the success of other women too often. This is a big mistake. United we stand, divided we fall. Mutual support and a natural support network are the only ways we can push everyone to succeed. We need to invent a sisterhood that will balance out the strength of male fraternity.

This has already begun. In California, there is a sisterhood that could inspire women elsewhere. When Odile Roujol settled in Silicon Valley, she was surprised not to see thousands of Sheryl Sandberg. The fact is, there is only a small number of women among partner venture capitalists who invest in startups and among entrepreneurs. A movement was founded in recent years to get things moving in the right direction and to raise awareness among men of the role that they also play if we want to avoid major cognitive bias in the tech world.

Her son Théophile got a bachelor's degree in computer science and is doing a PhD. The students come from every continent, but the number of women is limited. Education is key, to give girls more self-confidence, and attract them to scientific careers and the world of artificial intelligence, which will have an impact on our lives (education, health, transportation, etc.).

On the other hand, Odile is struck by the positive solidarity that unites women. A good example is Sukhinder Singh Cassidy, a former C-suite level executive at Google, founder of JOYUS, a video sales platform. She was born in Tanzania to Sikh parents and lived in Canada. Sukhinder is fighting for Silicon Valley businesses to have more inclusive governance and to take diversity into account. The Boardlist platform helps tech businesses to find candidates for their boards. For Sukhinder, women need to take leadership roles, bringing performance and creativity. And it is even better when those women are also from minority groups.

When Julie-Elya Hasson participated in an executive program at Stanford as a guest mentor, she worked with 29 entrepreneurs and only one was a woman. She had a front row seat to observe the scandals linked to investor sexism, and was notably very surprised to see investors asking more personal than professional questions. The positive side of this situation is the solidarity among women in this context. "I was often supported by women in the United States. They pushed me and helped me, even when they didn't really know me. That is what worked for me. I love being surrounded by women who are successful. I am very favorable to women's solidarity, which is often spontaneous and authentic, without specific expectation, because things balance out naturally and develop over time. Women's successes often go hand in hand with group successes. Women ask what they can do for others."

Barbara Belvisi feels a lot more benevolence for women now than she used to. Until recently, she had not felt support from other women but rather competition among women. However, the Hardware Club experience and her finance career changed her perspective. She now thinks that women will get more out of mutually supporting each other. "It is during difficult times that you feel female solidarity," she says. "You realize it exists, that what you are experiencing has happened to other women. The sisterhood is coming. Showing your vulnerability brings people together and is a sign of courage and maturity." Barbara tries to push her teams, to share her experience with younger women. Women need support, because they wear themselves out proving something to society, as if they need to do two times more to show their value. They are more subject to burnout than men, and tend to give of themselves so much they forget their own needs on the way.

It was a woman, Geneviève Petit, who introduced me to Clémentine Piazza. For the latter, real solidarity among women could be a solution to a lot of problems that we encounter today. One of the greatest challenges she faced came from a women, and her greatest allies are also women. Out of five people in her team, four are women. She admires how men help each other out and their solidarity, which has the same spirit as team sports, and she thinks that we are only at one on a scale of ten when it comes to female solidarity. "I do not see a lot of women around me who are involved in the success of other women, while men do it very naturally. I always ask the women I manage, 'Are you helping women out now?' You can always help someone. The good news is that the solution depends on us."

Willa

When we met Caroline Ramade in October 2017, she was still managing director of the incubator Paris Pionnières, which changed its name to Willa on March 8, 2018, for International Women's Day. "Pionnières" is the French word for pioneers, referring to women to tackle unknown territories. This notion has been at the heart of the NGO since it was founded on March 8, 2005. It seeks to be an accelerator of diversity and an invitation to hack the ecosystem.

Between 2005 and 2018, Paris Pionnières/Willa supported more than 450 startups with an exceptional rate of sustainability of 85 percent. It is the most diverse incubator in France. Its goal is not to be a female ghetto, but to get men and women together inventing tomorrow's solutions. Willa has a manifesto for inclusive growth that invites members to expand beyond the incubator to take wide-scale group action.

For Caroline, one of the levers of change lies in changing the fact that today women do not support each other enough. Knowing how to make place for other women and to stick together is a key to becoming strong. Caroline observes that women are good students, but that they don't ask each other for help enough and don't manage to partner well, or at all. Their lack of self-confidence does not create empathy or support. In the ecosystem she built with Paris Pionnières, she was very attentive to creating a real sisterhood. Sisterhood is about being available without expecting anything in return, about making connections between people. It is about raising up the women you really believe in. Caroline has spotlighted many women who were not part of the Paris Pionnières ecosystem. It is not by creating small groups of women who get together that we will change things. It is not about creating a stereotype of female entrepreneurs."

The incubator program was set up with these issues in mind. Pitching before you have a finished product is hard for women, because they tend to be perfectionists. There are personalized training courses with investors, both men and women, so they learn to ask for more money, because the average amount of funds raised by women is very low. Women learn better through their peers, and they take flight when they have a solid path. That is why Caroline set up experience-sharing meetings. "Let's stop trying to advance alone," she says. "We need to go find people and tell your story."

Caroline has recently launched a new venture called 50 in Tech (www.50intech.com) focusing on moving toward 50/50 gender equality in tech companies and gathering people from all other the world.

The Women Initiative Foundation

Founded in 2010 by Martine Liautaud, the Women Business Mentoring Initiative (WBMI) joined the Women Initiative Foundation (WIF) in 2016. It sets out to promote women in business and in the economy in general. Present both sides of the Atlantic, the foundation is developing more and more research and training. Annie Combelles runs the research department. She joined the WBMI when it was founding, after having met Martine Liautaud in 2010, following their joint nomination the Women Awards by *La Tribune*, a daily economic and finance newspaper. Annie never had a mentor because she never imagined that it could be possible, but today she mentors other women through the WIF.

Through her work in the foundation, she has observed that women set up their own obstacles, which she finds hard to understand. "I'm not the kind of person who is continually questioning myself. Do what you want to do, and if you meet a pitfall, you'll have the time to decide if you work around it or jump over it. You need to know how to seize an opportunity, and we all have just as many of them. If you work, you can do anything. There are things young women are afraid of. Many are alone, don't have associates, and end up throwing themselves on the first person to cross their path. They don't dare to ask for money. I was coaching a business that was doing well and needed working capital. The founder said to me, 'I'll be good with 700,000 euros.' I advised her to ask for more, because she wouldn't be able to ask for more later." Annie also observes that young women still think they need to be good at everything.

The WIF mentoring program focuses on businesses that are less than three years old, as there is a lot of aid available to companies in that phase, and it's not available later. The idea is to have long-term reasoning, which is what we do at The Refiners, where we warn startup founders that they are starting an adventure that will last five to ten years. I don't like the word "acceleration," which doesn't reflect this long-term notion. Sometimes, we need to decelerate a startup. The goal is to get them to help them lift their nose from the grindstone.

For that matter, Annie is very critical of the out-and-out fund raising culture, no matter the product or the service. This idea is taught in major business schools, when a company can succeed quite well without raising funds. In my opinion, we don't put enough stress on the difference between an investor providing some leverage at a given time and having cash.

StartHer

Magic Makers is an NGO that organizes coding workshops for children. During the event organized by Willa on March 8, 2018, Claude Terosier, the woman who founded the association, said that parents signed up more boys than girls for computer discovery workshops. Fanny Bouton (living proof you can be a girl and a geek) makes the same observation. She believe that France has a problem educating girls in digital technology. "Women from the association E-mma (which promotes diversity in technology) told me they had a hard time going to code because their mothers told them, 'It's not for you. You should be a beautician or go into retail work.' Coding is a unknown world seen as masculine territory. This preconceived idea is all the more wrong because at the beginning, women were working the coding machines. Men appropriated coding in the 1980s. Today, in France, the largest obstacles for girls learning coding is mothers." It all begins at home. When our own parents believe in our ambitions, it is easier to go for it. When she was a little girl, Frédérique Dame dreamed about being a business woman. When she asked her father what she needed to do to become one, her father said she'd need to go to business school, and her mother added, 'It's impossible. Nobody ever did that in the family.' In the end, Frédérique did it, as did her sister and her cousins, who followed her example.

Girls in Tech (GIT) is an international organization founded in 2007 in San Francisco with the goal of giving more visibility to women working in new technologies. It has over 100,000 members throughout the world and 60 local chapters. Roxanne Varza cofounded GIT Paris in 2010 with Mounia Rhka, and the British chapter in 2012 with Ella Wetson and Mihiri Bonney. When she started this project, she was writing for *TechCrunch* and was hungry to discover and write about more women. The only woman she had had the opportunity to talk about on the blog was Céline Lazorthe. Girls in Tech Paris organized different types of events that give women a platform to speak, such as conferences on various aspects of entrepreneurship. Since 2011, Lady Pitch Night is an open pitching competition for European tech startups with at least one woman in the founding team. In the United States, GIT organizes women-only events, but in France, the events are open to men, with the idea that inclusion is better for making change. The GIT team has also had men on it. For Roxanne, technology awareness begins at a very young age and mentalities are slow to evolve. When she was working at Microsoft, when middle school girls visited the premises, she noticed their distaste. They would say, 'This is just for boys who want to stay in front of the screen." And yet, Roxanne has seen a lot of women who wanted to start a business and couldn't because they didn't have enough tech savvy. Having notions about programming and coding can help anyone in any profession. Having basic knowledge about technical subjects help to communication and makes things smoother. GIT Paris also set up coding classes. In 2016, Girls in Tech Paris left the Girls in Tech network to become StartHer, because its projects were growing in the United States and their independence allowed them to go further. In the same movement, we can also mention Girlz in Web, a French association founded in 2009, to highlight women in digital technology. At the time I wrote this book, the French government was supporting the launch of a foundation to feminize digital professions.

Today, Roxanne manages Station F, the world largest startup campus, as CNBC recently called it. She observes that entrepreneurial flexibility is very appealing for both women and men, and she is seeing more and more startups founded by women. There are all kinds of women, including new graduates and women with more unusual paths like Jasmine Anteunis, an artist who did École 42, a teacher-less coding school in Paris, who at 25 co-founded Recast, a chatbot platform bought out by SAP in January 2018. The campus also sees more experienced women who have worked in large companies.

When Corinne Vigreux, the founder of TomTom, saw what Xavier Niel did with École 42, she was thrilled. She decided to license the teaching tool and open a similar school in Amsterdam, which is called

Codam. Corrine is passionate about social mobility and well placed to see the growing need for developers, and this project allowed her to combine the two. The school is mixed, of course, but she is trying to attract as many women as possible. Her objective is to reach a minimum of 40% women in the first class (compared with 10% at École 42).

Room for optimism

> *I have never supported women-only networks, but rather networks that include men and allow us to think about our cognitive biases together.*
>
> —Odile Roujol

Above, we mentioned only a few initiative among many programs that have emerged in recent years to support women and promote diversity in business and technology.

There are good reasons to be optimistic. Rania Belkahia, the founder of Afrimarket, is under 30 and doesn't see women of her generation being treated differently. Men and women who graduate from school are viewed the same. The new generation arriving on the labor market has ideas they want to try out and will dare to give them a try with few means. "It's interesting, because it will change the economic landscape," says Delphine Bellini. "Young women have their place in this new dynamic, because they are as creative, bold and resilient as men."

As dean of a major business school, Alice Guilhon has a front-row seat to watch the generations of students evolve, and she says that mentalities have completely changed. Students are more and more "big babies" and more and more ready to conquer the world. They are ready to make different career decisions than those before them, decisions richer in meaning. She says that 30 years ago, women censored themselves more, particularly when they were younger. Today, they are yearning for success and work-life balance. Around 2010, this quivering was perceptible, but young women still had reflexes such as getting up from the table to serve. The young women who are 20 today don't even have to demand that men get up too, it's natural. Openness and diversity are no longer a battle for them. The balance in their couple is no longer a problem. Millenials are marrying earlier. Family values are coming back, but in a more egalitarian form. Boys are looking for meaning in their careers, and not just to earn money in finance. They are on a quest for a balanced life. Children are no longer seen as slowing down a career. The social and solidarity economy is growing. Young people have projects that are more clear than they were 20 years ago.

Alice has a lot of confidence in this young generation she is helping to train. "I believe in transforming society through education. I have an incredible job. We accompany them to achieve their dreams and to be ambassadors of a new society. In addition to knowledge and values, we want to teach them critical thinking which was lost for 30 years as we all raced for the highest salaries. We want to teach them to ask questions. The students want to give meaning to a society that is breaking up. Young people are in a universe of sharing, of group consolidation. They are the ones pushing us to evolve, to remain open and aware. What is happening touches values, the system itself, and technology." At the heart of these changes in values, there is a place for women.

Chapter 7
Write Your Own Story

Conclusion

Shoot for the moon. Even if you miss, you'll land in the stars.

—Oscar Wilde

Don't hesitate to ask for help. Open your eyes: there is support all around you. Get out of your burrow. Go meet people. Try to understand what is happening in the ecosystem you want to enter. But keep in mind that all the support structures in the world will be of little help if you do not have a clear vision and if you haven't worked on yourself to remove your internal obstacles. Networks will bring a very valuable spark, but the catalyzer is you. It will also be very important to maintain the relationships that you make.

And what if you started by the end? You are the heroine of this book. I have tried not to give any lessons or provide coaching. I wanted to give you real, authentic experiences from our lives. I hope that the stories you have read in these pages have given you an impetus to move towards your dreams and the confidence in your ability to wipe away your doubts.

When I look back at the young woman I was when I founded B2L, I would certainly have advised her to depend more on herself than on her couple in making her professional choices, and that could backfire. I think young women today depend more on themselves, and that is all the better. I have three boys, but if I had a girl, I think I would tell her, "Try to think about your path and your independence, without being egotistical. Embrace opportunities without asking too many questions. Trust yourself and don't forget to build things that will allow you to flourish."

I found my work-life rhythm. It's up to you to find yours. As Adam Grant writes, "Work-life balance sets an unrealistic expectation of keeping different roles in steady equilibrium. Instead, strive for work-life rhythm. Each week has a repeating pattern of beats—job, family, friends, health, hobbies—that vary in accent and duration."

Inspiration

I asked the women you have met in this book what advice they would give to young women starting out. Like supplies for your journey, I leave you with some of their recommendations. Now, it's up to you to step it up and write your own story.

DELPHINE BELLINI

It is important to be proactive and to keep an open mind turned toward others. Everyone can build a project or rise in the ranks of an organization. You need to know how to expand your horizons by being interested in everything happening around you. This is a key element for doing your job. Knowledge, understanding, and respect are the pillars of success.

FANNY BOUTON

You need to know how to be humble. I try to learn all the time. I like to say I learn something new every day.

Also, you only have one life. I was lucky to understand this at a young age, twice. At 20, I had a car accident and I nearly died, which led me to say, 'Keep having fun.' Then, at the age of 30, when I had recently become a mother, due to a medical error the doctors told me I only had a few months left to live. I learned that I should take advantage of every second. You need money, but one can live on less. It is more interesting to surround yourself with smart, loving people. Nothing is more enriching than meeting people.

STÉPHANIE HOSPITAL

For a long time, I worked for men, and it didn't bother me to step aside to leave them the space. Then, I had a moment of awareness: you need to make sure you exist as well.

MYRIAM MAESTRONI

Watch over the quality of your relationships. We become like the people we spend time with. We all do the best we can, but not everyone is good to spend time with at a given time. The quality of your relationships can translate into peace, enthusiasm, and desire.

MARION MOREAU

You should always leave people a second (even a third or forth) chance.

CLÉMENTINE PIAZZA

Surround yourself with people who prefer nuance over principles, people who know that life is chaotic and that it can be delightful as it is. Ignore toxic people. Surround yourself with people who are benevolent, who are pirates, who are different. To blossom in who you are, you need to invite in difference.

ROXANNE VARZA

I often give these tips, which are valid for both men and women:

- Everyone wants to go to San Francisco, but for me France offered incredible opportunities. Changing countries or just looking elsewhere can be a great help.

- I am not convinced that it is always necessary to set up a startup. People often talk to me as if I had started my own business, although I never have. I set up a media, an association, a conference, but never a startup. We can have the same experiences with other types of projects. There is plenty to do, you can even start with a small project that can take off. There is a fad. Some people found businesses to found businesses, and not for the right reasons.

If you are doing business, be careful to keep cash. And above all, be passionate about what you do. Entrepreneurship is a difficult path, it takes a lot of resilience, do not see it as a fashionable lifestyle. Focus first on the problem you are solving.

AMIRA YAHYAOUI

I have three tips:

1. Smile! Be happy to be alive. What has helped me a lot in my life is to have understood early on the importance of being positive. I've been through extremely difficult times, and every time I had a problem, my dad would say, "In 20 years, it will be a story to tell." All the difficult things that happen to us will later become stories that will make you laugh. Twenty years later, we never tell a story about eating an excellent cake, we say that we ate a horrible cake filled with ants and we threw it all up. I believe that things are difficult at a given moment, but are not serious in hindsight. When something tough happens to me, I force myself to relativize it. I tell myself, 'In 20 years, how much will it have counted in my life? Not much. There are very few hard times in life that matter. And those are the only ones we should leave space for.

Being positive and smiling helped me more than mentors did. Being positive, seeing the good in people, not thinking that the other is silly, thinking that everyone can contribute good things and can open his mind. Opening yourself to opportunities will bring you more than you will lose.

2. Despite all the education your parents have given you, never apologize for existing. I am always getting backlash because I do not say "please." Thank, but do not beg.

3. Each of us has a definition of beauty—be it internal, external, alongside, or in front. Never give up beauty. The beauty of the soul, the beauty of the spirit, the beauty of what we do. I believe that women are powerful, and that we are able to do beautiful things with a more developed sense of beauty.

Useful Resources

The women in this book

MAÏA BAUDELAIRE
http://linkedin.com/in/maiabaudelaire

RANIA BELKAHIA
https://www.linkedin.com/in/raniabelkahia/

BARBARA BELVISI
http://linkedin.com/in/barbara-belvisi-79242118

ISABELLE BORDRY
http://linkedin.com/in/isabelle-bordry-75aa6913

FANNY BOUTON
http://linkedin.com/in/fannybouton

HELEN BOUYGUES
http://linkedin.com/in/helen-lee-bouygues-9b7601

MARION CARRETTE
http://linkedin.com/in/marion-carrette-65a41

ANNIE COMBELLES
http://linkedin.com/in/annie-combelles-1572905

FRÉDÉRIQUE DAME
http://linkedin.com/in/frederiquedame

RACHEL DELACOUR
http://linkedin.com/in/wearecloudrachel

HÉLÈNE DUVAL
http://linkedin.com/in/helene-duval-90a32b70

JULIE-ELYA HASSON
http://linkedin.com/in/hassonjulie

STÉPHANIE HOSPITAL
http://linkedin.com/in/stephaniehospital

MAËLLE GAVET
http://linkedin.com/in/maellegavet

ALICE GUILHON
http://linkedin.com/in/alice-guilhon-b6b68916

CÉLINE LAZORTHES
http://linkedin.com/in/lazorthes

GÉRALDINE LE MEUR
http://linkedin.com/in/geraldinelemeur

MYRIAM MAESTRONI
http://linkedin.com/in/myriammaestroni

MARION MOREAU
http://linkedin.com/in/marionmoreau

FANY PECHIODAT...
who is not on LinkedIn!

FLEUR PELLERIN
http://linkedin.com/in/fleurpellerin

CLÉMENTINE PIAZZA
http://linkedin.com/in/clémentine-piazza-42a67976

CAROLINE RAMADE
http://linkedin.com/in/carolineramade

ODILE ROUJOL
http://linkedin.com/in/odileroujol

MATHILDE THOMAS
http://linkedin.com/in/mathilde-thomas-32874886

ROXANNE VARZA
http://linkedin.com/in/roxannevarza

CORINNE VIGREUX
http://linkedin.com/in/corinnevigreux

SIBYLLE DE VILLENEUVE
http://linkedin.com/in/sibylle-de-villeneuve-384aa3

AMIRA YAHYAOUI
http://linkedin.com/in/amirayahyaoui

Initiatives

ALL RAISE
https://www.allraise.org/

THE BOARDLIST
www.theboardlist.com

FEMALE FOUNDERS COMMUNITY
https://www.facebook.com/groups/FemaleFoundersCommunity/

STARTHER
http://starther.org

SOCIAL BUILDER
http://socialbuilder.org

WILLA
http://hellowilla.co

WOMEN IN INNOVATION
http://winforumny.com

WOMEN INITIATIVE FOUNDATION
http://women-initiative-foundation.com

Find your *ikigai*!

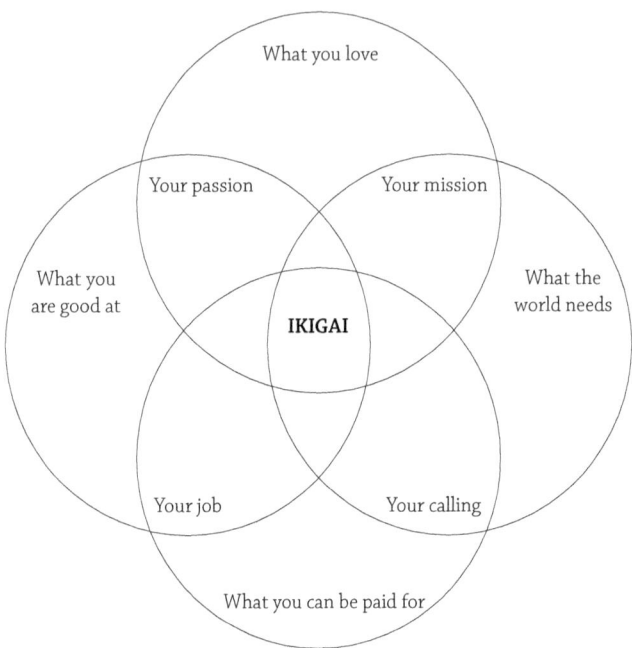

Steve Blank's business model canvas is another framework that could be useful to support your thought process if you have an entrepreneurial project: https://strategyzer.com/canvas/business-model-canvas.

See also, Cf. *The Startup Owner's Manual: The Step-By-Step Guide for Building a Great Company*, by Steve Blank and Bob Dorf.

Here is another lead for thinking about your work-life balance: http://safaribooksonline.com/library/view/business-model-you/9781118156315/09_chap03.html

Go further

Below are some references if you would like to look deeper into some of the topics covered in this book.

CHAPTER 1

For a full chronology of the Me Too movement, see Lydia Dishman, "This 'Me Too' Timeline Show Why 2017 Was a Reckoning for Sexism," *Fast Company*, 12/06/17:
http://fastcompany.com/40504569/this-me-too-timeline-shows-why-2017-was-a-reckoning-for-sexism.

See also:

- Sara Ashley O'Brien, 'I'm a creep. I'm Sorry." Another tech investor apologizes for mistreating women, *CNN Business*, 07/03/2017:
https://money.cnn.com/2017/07/02/technology/business/dave-mcclure-500-startups/index.html

- Katie Benner, "Women in Tech Speak Frankly on Culture of Harassment," *The New York Times*, 06/30/17:
https://www.nytimes.com/2017/06/30/technology/women-entrepreneurs-speak-out-sexual-harassment.html

- Marisa Kendall, "Silicon Valley now reeling in the wake of sexual harassment storm–After Uber, Binary Capital, 500 Startups scandals, 'People are realizing that it's not OK'," *The Mercury News*, 07/09/17:
http://mercurynews.com/2017/07/09/silicon-valley-reeling-wake-sexual-harassment-storm

- *Elephant in the Valley*, initiated by venture capitalist Trae Vassallo, among others.

- Emily Chang, Brotopia–Breaking Up the Boys' Club of Silicon Valley, Portfolio, 2018; Pui-Wing Tam, "How Silicon Valley Came to Be a Land of 'Bros," *The New York Times*, 02/05/18:
https://nytimes.com/2018/02/05/technology/silicon-valley-brotopia-emily-chang.html

For more on Susan Wojcicki:

- A. Pawlowski, "Why the YouTube CEO always tries to eat dinner with her kids, and 6 more things to know 2014," *Today*, 12/05/14: https://www.cnbc.com/2014/12/08/why-the-youtube-ceo-always-tries-to-eat-dinner-with-her-kids-and-6-more-things-to-know.html
- Susan Wojcicki, "Exclusive: How to Break Up The Silicon Valley Boys' Club," *Vanity Fair*, 03/16/17: https://www.vanityfair.com/news/2017/03/how-to-break-up-the-silicon-valley-boys-club-susan-wojcicki

On gender stereotypes and financial decisions: see November 2016 *ESSEC Knowledge* article, "Do gender stereotypes influence your financial decisions?" by François Longin and Estefania Santacreu-Vasut: http://knowledge.essec.edu/en/economy-finance/do-gender-stereotypes-influence-your-financial-dec.html

French articles and studies about women and professional success:

- Maëlle Lafond, "Une Française de moins de 30 ans sur deux prête à créer son entreprise," *Maddyness*, 03/22/18: https://www.maddyness.com/2017/10/10/etude-femmes-entrepreneuriat/
- Marina Al Rubbae, "La femme est-elle un dirigeant comme les autres ?" *Les Echos*, 10/09/15: https://business.lesechos.fr/entrepreneurs/aides-reseaux/dossiers/Femme-entrepreneur-/la-femme-est-elle-un-dirigeant-comme-les-autres-203527.php
- Iris Maignan, "Les femmes entrepreneures aussi performantes que les hommes?," *Maddyness*, 03/06/16: https://www.maddyness.com/2016/03/06/infographie-femmes-entrepreneures/
- *Les chiffres clés de l'entrepreunariat au féminin*, Anaxago, 01/30/18: https://www.anaxago.com/actualites/article/les-chiffres-cles-de-lentrepreunariat-au-feminin

- Morgane Miel, "Les trentenaires ne veulent plus faire carrière, mais...," *Madame Figaro*, 10/02/17: http://madame.lefigaro.fr/societe/les-trentenaires-ne-veulent-plus-faire-carriere-mais-250917-134390

On female founders:
- Valentina Zarya, "Female Founders Got 2% of Venture Capital Dollars in 2017," *Fortune*, 01/31/18: http://fortune.com/2018/01/31/female-founders-venture-capital-2017/

- Connie Loizos, "VC Aileen Lee just offered some very specific advice to female founders looking for funding," *TechCrunch*, 07/03/17: https://techcrunch.com/2017/07/03/vc-aileen-lee-just-offered-some-very-specific-advice-to-female-founders-looking-for-funding/

On Marissa Mayer:
- Jay Yarrow, "Sheryl Sandberg: Marissa Mayer Is Being Attacked Only Because She's A Woman," *Business Insider*, 03/08/13: https://www.businessinsider.fr/us/sheryl-sandberg-on-marissa-mayer-being-attacked-2013-3

- Bethany McLean, "Yahoo's Geek Goddess," *Vanity Fair*, 12/05/13: https://www.vanityfair.com/news/business/2014/01/marissa-mayer-yahoo-google

- Maya Kosoff, "The Inevitable Death of the Marissa Mayer Dream," *Vanity Fair*, 06/13/17: https://www.vanityfair.com/news/2017/06/the-inevitable-death-of-the-marissa-mayer-dream

- David Gelles, "Marissa Mayer Is Still Here," *The New York Times*, 04/18/18: https://www.nytimes.com/2018/04/18/business/marissa-mayer-corner-office.html

- Luke Stangel, "Marissa Mayer's next gig: Tech incubator Lumi Labs," *Bizwomen*: https://www.bizjournals.com/bizwomen/news/latest-news/2018/04/marissa-mayers-next-gig-tech-incubator-lumi-labs.html

Christine Lagarde at LeWeb in 2009–YouTube, 15/01/09:
https://www.youtube.com/watch?v=Lr5lkmBlGjc

On role modeling–Eva Pereira, "The Role Model Effect: Women Leaders Key To Inspiring The Next Generation," *Forbes*, 01/19/12: https://www.forbes.com/sites/worldviews/2012/01/19/the-role-model-effect-women-leaders-key-to-inspiring-the-next-generation/#15e9257d4fd2

On Etsy–Althea Erickson, "Data Show Etsy Sellers Driving a New Economy, First-Ever Microbusiness Caucus Launches on Capitol Hill," *Etsy News*, 28/03/17: https://blog.etsy.com/news/2017/data-show-etsy-sellers-driving-a-new-economy-first-ever-microbusiness-caucus-launches-on-capitol-hill/

Marion Moreau's interviews of over sixty players on the tech scene focusing on entrepreneurship. See *Accuraz, We Love Entrepreneurs Le film*, YouTube, 04/22/16: http://youtube.com/watch?v=o7wLfI25DLM

On digital assistants being female–Cale Guthrie Weissman, "Bank of America's bot is 'Erica' because apparently all digital assistants are women," *Fast Company*, 03/28/18. http://fastcompany.com/40551011/bank-of-americas-bot-is-erica-because-apparently-all-digital-assistants-are-women

CHAPTER 2

Women Initiative Foundation published a European study on stereotypes and the perception of diversity in large corporations: http://women-initiative-foundation.com/fr/2018/03/09/3-avril-2018/

See also this tragic and edifying article by Ariana Eunjung Cha, "The struggle to conceive with frozen eggs," *The Washington Post*, 01/27/18: https://www.washingtonpost.com/news/national/wp/2018/01/27/feature/she-championed-the-idea-that-freezing-your-eggs-would-free-your-career-but-things-didnt-quite-work-out/

See Ophélie Ostermann's "Charge mentale: Le perfectionnisme domestique étouffe les femmes," *Madame Figaro*, 02/07/18 http://madame.lefigaro.fr/bien-etre/charge-mentale-bd-emma-interview-psychiatre-aurelia-schneider-livre-070218-146891

If you tend to procrastinate, see the TED talk "Inside the Mind of a Master Procrastinator": ted.com/talks/ tim_urban_inside_the_mind_of_a_master_procrastinator

For a good matrix to help define your priorities, see Brett McKey and Kate McKey, *The Eisenhower Decision Matrix: How to Distinguish Between Urgent and Important Tasks* and "Make Real Progress in Your Life," *The Art of Manliness*, 10/23/13: https://www.artofmanliness.com/articles/eisenhower-decision-matrix/

For checklists, I recommend reading *The Checklist Manifesto: How to Get Things Right* by Atul Gawande (Metropolitan Books, 2009).

Ikigai comes from *ikiru*, to live, and *kai*, "the result of hope." The combination means "a reason to live and get up in the morning." Find out more in Tom Ough's "Finding your Ikigai: The Japanese Secret to Health and Happiness," *Telegraph*, 07/16/17. https://www.telegraph.co.uk/health-fitness/mind/finding-ikigai-japanese-secret-health-happiness/

On objectives and key results, see the book by the John Doerr, published in April 2018, *Measure What Matters: How Google, Bono, and the Gates Foundation Rock the World with OKRs* (Penguin Random House).

Myriam Maestroni did a lot of work on customer relations. She wrote a book with Luis-Maria Huette on a Harvard model, *Intelligence émotionnelle, services et croissance* (Maxima, 2009).

Chapter 3

On women and the imposter syndrome: Mariam Naficy, "#SheBrag", Medium: https://medium.com/@naficy/shebrag-98be0eedb9df.
See Margaret Neale's negotiations course at Stanford.

"The Top 20 Reasons Startups Fail," *CB Insights*, 02/02/18:
http://cbinsights.com/research/startup-failure-reasons-top

Evan Williams in one of the last Masters of Scale podcasts, "Never underestimate your first idea":
mastersofscale.com/ev-williams-never-underestimate-your-first-idea-2

Rachel Delacour, Female Founders office hours: Prochaine édition à Station F, July 2, LinkedIn, 06/11/18:
http://linkedin.com/pulse/female-founders-office-hours-prochaine-edition-a-station-delacour

CHAPTER 4

Emily Livorsi, "Eight Characteristics of Agile Leaders," *FMI*, 09/01/16:
http://fminet.com/fmi-quarterly/article/2016/09/eight-characteristics-of-agile-leaders

CHAPTER 5

Cf. this tweet from David Hornik on July 10, 2017: "I'm increasingly convinced that all startup CEOs should have a coach with whom she can be fully transparent and work through tough problems.":
http://twitter.com/davidhornik/status/884116616476106752

Atul Gawande, the author of *The Checklist Manifesto* (op.cit.), also wrote an excellent article in 2011–"Personal Best: Top Athletes and Singers Have Coaches. Should you?" (*The New Yorker*, 10/03/11):
http://newyorker.com/ magazine/2011/10/03/personal-best

For French statistics–Baromètre StartHer-KPMG–Les levées de fonds des startup Tech dirigées par des femmes en 2017, KPMG, 03/21/17:
https://home.kpmg/fr/fr/home/media/press-releases/2017/02/barometre-starther-levees-fonds-start-up-dirigees-par-des-femmes.html

Acknowledgements

A project became reality. I thank all of you for having trusted me. Without you, this book would not have seen the day.

I thank my French publisher, Dominique, for coming to look for me and introducing me to Anaïs.

Anaïs, thank you for the great work we have done together and this great collaboration.

Anne, thank-you for your awesome work on the English version of this book.

Thank you to all the people with whom I have been fortunate to collaborate for the last 20 years, including my LeWeb dream team: Christophe, Pascal, Bastien, Morgan, Miriam, Florence, Sabine, Karyn, Boris, to name a few.

Thank you to my friends who are important to me. I did not interview them all, and yet they also had their place in this book. I am thinking in particular of Beatrice, Laure, Estelle, Barbara, Carole, Cecile, Fidji, and many others.

Thanks to Gregory for the artificial intelligence French title search boost.

A huge thank you to Alexandre for the beautiful preface. The voice of a man was important because, gentlemen, this book is also dedicated to you, even if I did not really give you the floor.

I would like to also tip my hat to Cheyenne and Géraldine. Go for it, girls, a bright future awaits you.